D0935150

MUSIC OF THE MINNESINGER AND EARLY MEISTERSINGER

UNIVERSITY OF NORTH CAROLINA
STUDIES IN THE GERMANIC LANGUAGES
AND LITERATURES

NUMBER THIRTY-TWO

UNIVERSITY
OF NORTH CAROLINA
STUDIES IN
THE GERMANIC LANGUAGES
AND LITERATURES

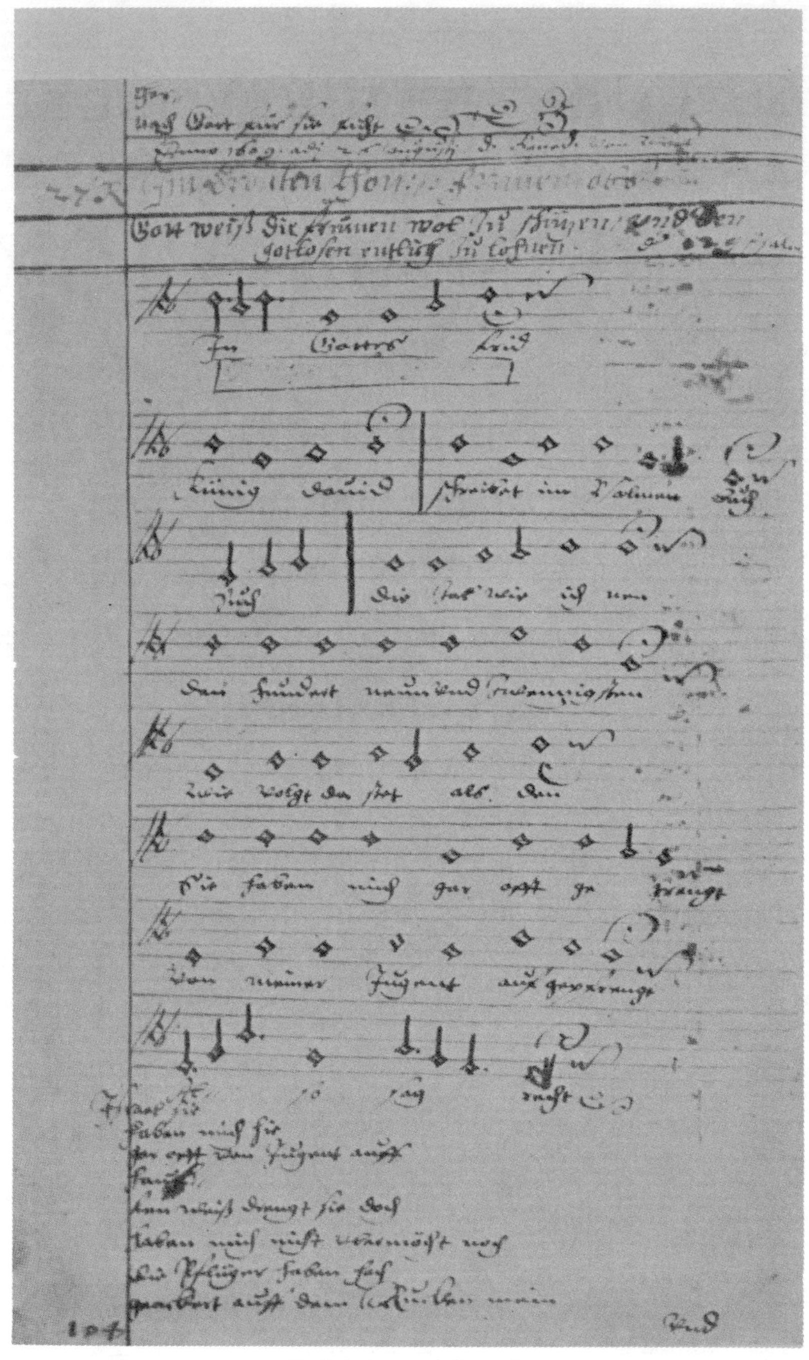

Berlin, Germ. Fol. 24, f. 224v.

MUSIC OF THE MINNESINGER AND EARLY MEISTERSINGER

A BIBLIOGRAPHY

BY

ROBERT WHITE LINKER

AMS PRESS INC.
New York
1966

Reprinted with the permission of
the original publisher

AMS PRESS, INC.
New York, N.Y. 10003
1966

Manufactured in the United States of America

TO

FOUR GENERATIONS OF

GOOD FRIENDS

GENE, BOYKIN, LARRIE, EUGENE

PREFACE

The study of the songs of the Minnesinger is complicated by the fact that most of the tunes have come down to us only in late manuscripts, with the original *Ton* or *Weise* accompanied by new texts by later poets, leaving questions of authenticity or corruption to be solved. In addition to this, histories of mediaeval music frequently treat as Minnesinger certain poets whom the historian of literature considers as Meistersinger. I have not attempted to settle this disagreement, but have included both groups, with dates, wherever available, to distinguish between the earlier Minnesinger and the later Meistersinger.

The bibliography is arranged alphabetically by composer, with each of his songs in alphabetical order following any general work on the composer. It will be noted that the same tune may occur a number of times, with different words. Perhaps I should have eliminated this multiple use, but since many of these entries have become part of musical literature, I have presented them as found. Under each song is listed, where pertinent and available to me, the manuscript and folio, any ascription or designation of tune contained in the manuscript, publication, with reproduction of mediaeval notation designated by ¶, transcription into modern notation by ♩. Occasionally I have cited editions of the text without music.

The list of manuscripts at the beginning of the book gives general facts on the manuscript, and any publication or facsimile reproduction. Thereafter the manuscripts are cited by place and number, or the more extensive manuscripts such as the Colmar or Jena by name. After the list of manuscripts is given a list of publications with the abbreviations used for them.

There are doubtless many shortcomings to this bibliography, chief among which is the need for re-assignment to the original words of tunes borrowed by later writers, yet I hope that an orderly listing will be of use to students of German literature and music.

No collection of material such as this would have been possible without the help of my friends and the libraries I have secured materials from. Among the many who have helped, I should like especially to thank Professor John G. Kunstmann for the use of his books and his knowledge, Miss Thelma Thompson and Mr. Keith Mixter for numerous friendly aids, Dr. Ewald Jammers of Heidelberg, Dr. Wilhelm Virneisel of Tübingen, for their very generous checking and securing for me basic materials. Lastly, I am very grateful to my fellow alumni, whose financial assistance, through the University Research Council, have made publication possible.

Chapel Hill, N.C., 6 February, 1961 RWL

MANUSCRIPTS

The greatest of the manuscripts of the poetry of the Minnesinger is the Manesse, or Grosse Heidelberger: Heidelberg, Universitätsbibliothek, Cod. Pal. Germ. 848. Copiously illustrated with Minnesinger portraits and scenes, but without music. It has been reproduced in facsimile by the Inselverlag, Leipzig, 1925-29.

MUSIC

1. Bartsch's fragment: *See* 60-5.
2. Basel, Universitätsbibliothek, Fragmentenband, N.J. 3, nr. 145. *See* 17 (Meister Kelin), 53 (Vegeviur), *and* JHSB II, 154.
3. Berlin, Preussische Staatsbibliothek, Ms. germ. fol. 24. Paper, XVI C. Meisterlieder, including Minnesinger tunes. 277ff. Fol. 223 begins old series of numbers as f.1. *See* HM IV, 907, nos. 64-67; *also non-musical manuscripts below*. (*Now in* Tübingen: *see 5 below*.
4. Berlin, Preussische Staatsbibliothek, Ms. germ. fol. 25 (*Now in* Tübingen, *see 5 below*). XVI C. 460 pp. *See* HM IV, 907, nos. 64-7.
5. Berlin, Preussische Staatsbibliothek, Ms. germ. fol. 779,ff. 131-269. (*Now* Tübingen, Universitätsbibliothek, Depot der ehem. Preuss. Staatsbibliothek. Ms. germ. fol. 779) Friedrich von der Hagen's Neidhart manuscript. Facsimile: W. Schmieder, DTO LXXI (1930), 3-20, 31-39. *See further*: Keinz, *Beiträge zur Neidhartforschung*, Bayr.Sitz.-Ber., Phil.-hist. Kl. (1888), II, 312. Brill, *Die Schule Neidharts*, 45ff. Haupt-Wiessner, *Neidhart von Reuenthal*, VIII ff.
6. Berlin, Preussische Staatsbibliothek, Ms. germ.fol. 922. XV C. Music, ff. 131-34. (*Now* Tübingen, Universitätsbibliothek: *see 5 above*). Margarete Lang, *Zwischen Minnesang und Volkslied. Die Lieder der Berliner Hs. germ. fol. 922. Die Weisen bearbeitet von Joseph M. Müller-Blattau* (Studien zur Volksliedforschung, hrsg. von John Meier, Heft 1. Berlin, 1941). Carl von Kraus, *Zu den Liedern der Berliner Hs.germ. fol. 922*, / Abhandlungen der Bayer. Akad. d. Wissenschaft, Phil.-hist. Abtlg., N.F., Heft 21, München, 1942.
7. Berlin, Preussische Staatsbibliothek, Ms. germ. 4°, 981. *Now* Westdeutsche Bibliothek, Marburg). One folio, parchment, from Magdeburger Archiv. Facsimile, HM IV, 773; Wolf, *Handbuch der Notationskunde*. *See* 60-2.

- Breslau: *See* Wrocław.
- Colmar: *See* München.

8. Donaueschingen, Fürstlich-Fürstenbergische Bibliothek, Hs. 120. XV-XVI C.
Runge, *Die Sangesweisen der Colmarer Handschrift und Liederhandschrift Donaueschingen*. Leipzig, Breitkopf und Härtel, 1896.
Karl Bartsch, *Meisterlieder*, 89ff., gives a table of contents.
9. Engelberg Ms. *See* 26-1.
10. Erlangen, Universitätsbibliothek, Ms. 1655. XV C. Paper. 14 ff.
See HM IV, 904a.
11. Frankfurt-am-Main, Staatsbibliothek, Neidhart fragment, 2 ff.
See HM IV, 770-71. Facsimile, DTO LXXI.
12. Heidelberg, Universitätsbibliothek, Hs. 329.
See 15 (Hugo von Montfort).
13. Innsbruck, Universitätsbibliothek.
See 31 (Oswald von Wolkenstein).
14. Jena, Universitätsbibliothek, Jenaer Liederhandschrift. Facsimile: K. K. Müller, *Die Jenaer Liederhandschrift in Lichtdruck*. Jena, 1896. Holz, Saran, Bernoulli, *Die Jenaer Liederhandschrift*, Leipzig, Hirschfeld, 1901. 2 vols. Karl Bartsch, *Untersuchung zur Jenaer Liederhandschrift* (Palaestra 140). Leipzig, 1923. Karl B. Brandis, „Zur Entstehung und Geschichte der Jenaer Liederhandschrift", *Z.f. Bücherfreunde* XXI, 108. E. Jammers, „Untersuchungen über die Rhytmik und Melodik der Melodien der Jenaer Liederhandschrift", ZfMW VII (1924-25), 265-304. HM IV, reproduction of original notation.
– Kolmar: *See* München.
15. Königsberg, Univ. Bibl. 7 ff. *See* 8-7.
16. Kremsmünster, Stiftsbibliothek, Ms. 127, VII, 18, f. 130 ab. *See* Franz Pfeiffer, *Germania* II (1857), 470.
17. Leipzig, Universitätsbibliothek, ms. 1305, ff. 107-110.
See 19 (Konrad von Queinfurt).
– Magdeburg, Archiv: *See* Berlin 981.
Facsimile: HM IV, 773
18. München, Staatsbibliothek, Cod. germ. 4997. Paper. XV C.
The Colmar Manuscript.
Paul Runge, *Die Sangesweisen der Colmarer Handschrift und die Liederhandschrift Donaueschingen*. Leipzig, Breitkopf und Härtel, 1896. Friedrich Ebert, *Die Liedweisen der Kolmarer Handschrift und ihre Einordnung und Stellung in der Entwicklungsgeschichte der deutschen Liedweise im* 14. *bis* 16. *Jahrhundert*. 114 pp. Diss. Göttingen, 1933. Rudolf Zitzmann, *Die Melodien der Kolmarer Liederhandschrift*. Würzburg, Triltsch, 1944. Karl Bartsch, *Meisterlieder der Kolmarer Handschrift*. Stuttgart, Bibliothek des litterarischen Vereins in Stuttgart, LVIII, 1862. Heinz Otto Burger, *Die Kunstauffassung der frühen Meistersinger, ein Untersuchung über die Kolmarer Handschrift*. Berlin, Junker und Dünnhaupt, 1936. 80 pp.

19. München, Staatsbibliothek, Cgm. 5249/32. Fragment. *See* 8-7. München fragment M: Facsimile in Eduard Bernoulli, *Die Choralnotenschrift bei Hymnen und Sequenzen*. Leipzig, Breitkopf u. Härtel, 1898.
20. München, Staatsbibliothek, Clm. 5509. Lost.
See KLD, pp. XXI-XXII.
21. München, Staatsbibliothek, Clm. 5530.
22. München, Staatsbibliothek, Clm. 5539.
See 49-4.
23. München, Docen, fragment of Walther von der Vogelweide.
See HM IV, 901, no. 10 Lost.
24. München, Staatsbibliothek, Cod. Lat. 4660 (Carmina Burana).
See KLD, p. XIX; *also* 30-16.
25. Münster, Staatsarchiv, Ms. VII, 51. Fragment, 4 pp., five songs, only one complete. XIV-XV C.
R. F. Molitor, „Die Lieder des Münsterischen Fragmentes," SIMG XII (1910-11), 475-500, bibliography, 475, facsimile, 500ff. F. Jostes, „Bruchstück einer Münsterschen Minnesängerhandschrift, mit Noten", zfdA LIII (1912), 348-57.
26. Nürnberg, Stadtbibliothek, Ms. 784: *see* 57-6.
27. Nürnberg, Stadtbibliothek, Ms. 792: *see* 57-6.
28. Schreiber fragment. Lost.
H. Schreiber, *Taschenbuch f. Geschichte und Altertum in Süddeutschland*, 1838; HM IV, 772; Hugo Kuhn, *Minnesangs Wende*, Tübingen, 1952. Facsimile in all three.
See 50-1.
– Sterzing: *See* Vipiteno.
29. Stettin, Schulbibliothek. Fragment.
See HM IV, 904, no. 39; HM IV, 769, Tafel V.
30. Strassburg.
See 32-2.
31. Trier, Stadtbibliothek, Hs. 724. XV C.
See 32-2.
32. Vipiteno, Stadtarchiv.
See 30 (Neidhart von Reuenthal) *and* H. Rietsch, *Die deutsche Liedweise* (1904), p. 215f. Facsimile, DTO LXXI.
33. Wien, Nationalbibliothek, Hs. 2701. Paper. XIV C.
HM IV, 768, 769, 774. H. Rietsch, DTO XLI, facsimile and transcription. G. Roethe, *Reinmar von Zweter*, 147f.
34. Wien, Nationalbibliothek, Hs. 2777.
See 31 (Oswald von Wolkenstein) *and* DTO XVIII.
35. Wien, Nationalbibliothek, Hs. 2856 (Mondseer Hs.).
See 13-4, 13-10 and *Germanica* III-IV.
36. Wien, Nationalbibliothek, ms. suppl. 3344.
See 30 (Neidhart von Reuenthal), and DTO LXXI. Facsimile, DTO LXXI.

37. Wien, Nationalbibliothek, Titurel Hs. 40 (Ambr. 421).
HM IV, 774; facsimile, HM IV, 903, no. 30.
38. Wien, K. K. Fideicommissbibliothek, Cod. membr. 7970.
See 32-2.
39. Wrocław, Biblioteka Universytecka, Ms. 356. Adam Puschman's *Singebuch. Reported lost during World War II.*
See partial publication below, under APSB.
40. Wrocław, Bibl. Univ., Ms I.Q. 368.
See 8-7, *and* Paul Pietsch, ZfdP XIV (1882), 98-99.

NON-MUSICAL MANUSCRIPTS

Frequently mentioned in connection with the Minnesinger are, among others, the following manuscripts containing poetic texts, but without notation of music:
Berlin, Staatsbibliothek, Hss. germ. f°, 22 and 23. (Now in Tübingen). *See* 5 *above.*
Heidelberg, Universitätsbibliothek, Hss. 109, 392, and 680.

PUBLICATIONS

General:

1. Archer Taylor, *The Literary History of Meistergesang.* New York, Modern Language Association of America, 1937.
2. Karl Goedeke, *Grundriss zur Geschichte der deutschen Dichtung aus den Quellen.* Dresden, Ehlermann, 1884.
3. *Die deutsche Literatur des Mittelalters. Verfasser Lexikon.* Vols. I-II, ed. Wolfgang Stammler; III-V, ed. Karl Langosch. Berlin, Walter de Gruyter & Co.
4. TEBM: Archer Taylor and Frances H. Ellis, *A Bibliography of Meistergesang.* Indiana University Studies, XXIII, 1936. Pp. 92.

Music and Texts:

5. Ursula Aarburg, „Melodien zum frühen deutschen Minnesang," zfdA LXXXVII (1956-57), 24-45.
6. AfMw: *Archiv für Musikwissenschaft.*
7. APSB: G. Münzer, *Das Singebuch des Adam Puschman nebst den Originalmelodien.* Leipzig, Breitkopf und Härtel, 1906, 96 pp. Melodies published, in modern notation, indicated below by ♩.
8. BMKH: Karl Bartsch, *Meisterlieder der Kolmarer Handschrift.* Bibliothek des litterarischen Vereins in Stuttgart, LXVIII, Stuttgart, 1862.

9. DAHA: Archibald T. Davison and Willi Apel, *Historical Anthology of Music*, Vol. I. Harvard University Press, 1947.
10. DTO: Denkmäler der Tonkunst in Österreich. DTO XLI: *Gesänge von Frauenlob, Reinmar v. Zweter und Alexander, nebst einem anonymen Bruchstück nach der Handschrift 2701 der Wiener Hofbibliothek bearbeitet von Heinrich Rietsch mit Reproduction der Handschrift.* Wien, Artaria, 1913.
    DTO XVIII: *see* Oswald von Wolkenstein.
    DTO LXXI: *see* Neidhart von Reuenthal.
11. GFML: Friedrich Gennrich, *Grundriss einer Formelehre des mittelalterl. Liedes.* Halle, Niemeyer, 1932.
12. Fr. Gennrich, „Liedkontrafactur in Mhd. und ahd. Zeit," ZfdA LXXXII (1948), 105-41.
13. Fr. Gennrich, „Mittelalterliche Lieder mit textloser Melodie," AfMw IX (1952), 120ff.
14. Friedrich Gennrich, *Melodien altdeutscher Lieder.* Darmstadt, 1954.
15. Fr. Gennrich, *Mittelhochdeutsche Liedkunst.* Darmstadt, 1954.
16. Fr. Gennrich, *Übertragungsmaterial zur Rhythmik der Ars Antiqua.* Darmstadt, 1954.
17. GMMA: Théodor Gérold, *La Musique au moyen âge.* Paris, Cfmâ, Champion, 1932.
18. GTM: Friedrich Gennrich, *Troubadours, Trouvères, Minne- und Meistergesang.* Köln, Volk, 1951, 1960.
19. HGEM: Harold Gleason, *Examples of Music before 1400.* New York, Crofts, 1946. 117 pp.
20. HM: Friedrich von der Hagen, *Minnesinger.* 5 vols. Leipzig, Barth, 1838. Vol. IV contains bibliography of Minnesinger manuscripts, facsimiles, and reproduction of original notation of Jena manuscript (pp. 775-844), and of the songs of Neidhart (pp. 845-852).
21. JHSB: Holz, Saran, Bernoulli, *Die Jenaer Liederhandschrift.* 2 vols. Leipzig, Hirschfeld, 1901.
22. KLD: Carl von Kraus, *Deutsche Liederdichter des 13. Jahrhunderts.* Tübingen, Niemeyer, 1952.
23. Kuhn-Reichert: Hugo Kuhn, *Minnesang des 13. Jahrhunderts... mit Übertragung der Melodien von* Georg Reichert. Tübingen, Niemeyer, 1953. Pp. 160.
24. Lang-Salmen: Margarete Lang, *Ostdeutscher Minnesang...* Melodien hrsg. v. Walter Salmen. Lindau, Kostanz, Thorbecke, 1958.
25. MGDM: Hans Joachim Moser, *Geschichte der deutschen Musik.* Stuttgart, Berlin, Cotta, 1930.
26. NOHM: *The New Oxford History of Music.* Vol. II, *Early Medieval Music up to 1300.* Oxford University Press, 1954.
27. PC: Alfred Pillet, Henry Carstens, *Bibliographie der Troubadours.* Halle, Niemeyer, 1933.

28. PMDL: Fridrich Pfaff, *Der Minnesang des 12. bis 14. Jahrhunderts.* (Deutsche National-Literatur, VIII). Stuttgart, Union, *ca.* 1890.
29. Riemann: Hugo Riemann, *Handbuch der Musikgeschichte*, I, 2, *Die Musik des Mittelalters.* Leipzig, Breitkopf und Härtel, 1905.
30. RMMA: Gustave Reese, *Music in the Middle Ages.* New York, Norton, 1940.
31. SGMB: Arnold Schering, *Geschichte der Musik in Beispielen.* Leipzig, Breitkopf und Härtel, 1931.
32. SIMG: *Sammelbände der Internationalen Musikgesellschaft.*
33. *Das Taghorn. Dichtungen und Melodien des Bayrisch-Oesterreichischen Minnesanges*, ed. Alfred Rottauscher und B. Paumgartner. 3 vols. Wien, 1922.
34. Ronald J. Taylor, „Zur Übertragung der Melodien der Minnesänger," ZfdA LXXXVII (1956-57), 132-47.
35. Otto Ursprung, „Vier Studien zur Geschichte des deutschen Liedes," I. „Mein traut gesell, mein liebster Hort, ein neujahrslied aus ca. 1300," *Archiv für Musikwissenschaft* IV (1922), 413-19. II. „Die Mondseer Liederhandschrift und Herman, der Münch von Salzburg," V (1923), 11-30. *See* 14-10.
36. F. Vogt, *Des Minnesangs Frühling*, Leipzig, Hirzel, 1888. (30 Aufl. 1950).
37. Johann Christof Wagenseil, *Buch von der Meistersinger holdseligen Kunst*... Pp. 433-575 of his *De Sacri Rom. Imperii libera Civitate Noribergensi Commentatio.* Nuremberg, 1697.
38. Wehrli: Max Wehrli, *Deutsche Lyrik des Mittelalters.* Zürich, Manesse Verlag, 1955.
39. ZfdA: *Zeitschrift für deutsches Altertum und deutsche Literatur.*
40. ZfMW: *Zeitschrift für Musikwissenschaft.*
41. Zitzmann: Rudolf Zitzmann, *Die Melodien der Kolmarer Liederhandschrift.* Würzburg, Triltsch, 1944.

Further bibliography, dealing with relations of Minnesinger, Trouveres, and Troubadours, listed under 61.

1. DER WILDE ALEXANDER

(Meister Alexander)

XIII C

Rudolf Haller, *Der wilde Alexander*. Würzburg, Triltsch, 1935
Gunther Hase, *Der Minneleich Meister Alexanders*. Halle, 1921.
DTO XLI

1. **Ach owê, daz nâch liebe ergât**
   Jena 25b; Wien 2701, f. 49
   HM IV, 785 ♪; JHSB I, 46 ♪, II, 14 ♩, 113 ♩; DTO XLI, 86 ♩
   CE: KLD I, 13

2. **Ein wunder in der werlde vert**
   Jena 22a
   HM IV, 783 ♪; JHSB I, 41 ♪, II, 12 ♩
   CE: KLD I, 2

– Ein trurechiches...: 1-4

3. **Hie vor dô wir kinder wâren**
   Jena 24d
   HM IV, 784 ♪; JHSB I, 46 ♪, II, 13 ♩, 118 ♩; GTM III, 8 ♩; GMMA 220 ♩; Kuhn-Reichert 153 ♩
   HM III, 30; Wehrli, 435; CE: KLD I, 12

4. **Min trûreclîchez klagen**
   Wien: „Das ist des wildyn Alexandyrs leych"
   Jena 25d; Wien 2701, f. 44
   HM IV, 785-90 ♪; JHSB I, 47 ♪, II, 14 ♩; DTO XLI, 83-86 ♩; Kuhn-Reichert 154 ♩
   HM II, 364-65; CE: KLD I, 15
   Stanza 11: Nu memet war, diz ist der schilt
   MGDM I, 173 ♩
   Leich

5. **Siôn trûre**
   Jena 24b
   HM IV, 784 ♪; JHSB I, 45 ♪, II, 13 ♩; MGDM I, 167 ♩
   HM III, 30; CE: KLD I, 10

2. MEISTER ANKER

XIV C

TEBM 29; BMKH 181

1. **Heiliger geist, din kraft mit aller guete**
   „In meister Anckers tone"
   Colmar 779
   Runge, Colmar, 167 ♪
   BMKH 548

3. MEISTER BOPPE

XIII C

TEMB 30-31; BMKH 166. Meister Boppe and Der Starke Boppe (XIV C) often confused.
G. Tolle, *Der Spruchdichter Boppe, Versuch einer kritischen Ausgabe seiner Dichtungen.* Progr. Sondershausen, 1894

1. **Ich weiss nit, ob der hymmel hanget oder swebt**
   „Gesang in dez starcken Boppen hofedone"
   Colmar 555; APSB 60
   Runge, Colmar, 136 ♪; JHSB II, 197 ♩
   H. Enke, „Der 'hofedon' des Meister Boppe", *Festschrift für Max Schneider.* Leipzig, 1955.

2. **O hoer unde starker almechtiger Got**
   Jena 111c
   HM IV, 831 ♪; JHSB I, 192 ♪, II, 69 ♩;
   Runge, Colmar, 137 ♪
   PMDL I, 217

– BURK MANGOLT –

Composer of music to poems of Hugo von Montfort, *q.v.*

– EHRENBOTE VOM RHEIN: *see* REINMAR VON ZWETER –

– FRAUENLOB: *see* HEINRICH VON MEISSEN –

4. MEISTER FRIEDRICH VON SUNNENBURG

2/2 XIII C

1. **Ein richer kunik hiez Kosdras**
   Jena 70b
   HM IV, 807 ♪; JHSB I, 119 ♪, II, 40 ♩

2. **Ich wil singen**
Jena 72d
HM IV, 808 ♪ ; JHSB I, 123 ♪ , II, 42 ♩
HM III, 78

3. **Nu merke ho und edele man**
Jena 71b
HM IV, 808 ♪ ; JHSB I, 121 ♪ , II, 41 ♩

4. **O wol dir, Welt, o wol dir hiute und je mermere wol**
Jena 63c
HM IV, 806 ♪; JHSB I, 108 ♪ , II, 39 ♪

See also 20-2

5. MEISTER GERVELIN

1. **Drivaltik name der Goteheit**
Jena 31b
HM IV, 792 ♪ ; JHSB I, 58 ♪ , II, 21 ♩
HM III, 35

2. **Golt von Arabie ist guot, daz darf ouch nieman strafen**
Jena 35b
HM IV, 792 ♪ ; JHSB I, 61 ♪ , II, 22 ♩
HM III, 37

6. DER GUTER

XIII C

1. **Hie vor ein werder ritter lak**
Jena 38b-39a
HM IV, 794 ♪ ; JHSB I, 67 ♪ , II, 24 ♩ ;
HM III, 41

7. HARDER, KONRAD

XIV-XV C

BMKH 182

1. **Ayn schone meit dorchsonet**
„In des Harders korwyse, der guldin schilling, ist ein leych"
Colmar 33
Runge, Colmar, 20 ♪
BMKH 192

2. **Man höret aber richen schal**
„Des Harders guldin rey"
Colmar 36
Runge, Colmar, 20
BMKH 197

3. **Mary, kungynn ob allen kunne**
„In dem Harder sin hoffwyse"
Colmar, 845; APSB 90, „süsse ton"
Runge, Colmar, 183

8. HEINRICH VON MEISSEN (FRAUENLOB)

1260-1318

TEBM 36; DTO XLI; BMKH 168-75
L. Ettmüller, *Heinrichs von Meissen des Frauenlobes Leiche, Sprüche, Streitgedichte und Lieder.* Quetlinburg und Leipzig, 1843. Helmuth Thomas, *Untersuchungen zur Überlieferung der Spruchdichtung Frauenlobs.* (Palaestra 217). Leipzig, 1939. Mss., pp. 2-146.
A. E. Kroeger, *The Lay of Our Lady. Translated from the German of Frauenlob.* St. Louis, 1877. Ludwig Pfannmüller, *Frauenlobs Marienleich.* Strassburg, Trübner, 1913. Margarete Lang, *Der Minnesinger Frauenlob.* Mainz, 1951. Kirsch, *Frauenlobs Kreuzleich.* Diss. Dillingen, 1930. H. Enke, „Der vergessene Ton Frauenlobs", *Musikforschung* IV (1951). K. H. Bertau, R. Stephan, „Wenig beachtete Frauenlobfragmente," ZfdA LXXXVI (1955-56), 302-20.

TONES

Anckelwyse 21
Blauen 3
Bluenden 23
Frauenleich 7
Froschwyse 9
Dan 18
Gecronten 13, 41, 44, 56
Geilen 4
Geschwinden 24
Gruenen 1, 16, 38, 53
Gruntwys 11
Gulden 31
Gulden Radweise 35, 51
Hagenblu 49
Heylygin crucys leich 55
Hunds Fuss 57
Huntwyse 36
Jar Weiss 15
Kupfer 32
Langen 25, 29
Leit 12
Mynnekliche leych 42
Newen 33, 52
Ritter Weiss 22, 37
Slosshort 27
Spätten 26
Spiegelwyse 30, 50
Spruch 19, 20, 39, 40, 43
Suessen 10
Tagweiss 34
Thon thon 58
Überzarten 14
Vergessnen 2, 48
Verholn 5
Vluk 46
Würgindrossil 6, 8, 54
Zarten 17, 28, 45
Zugweiss 47

1. **Alle so hie betrüglich**
„In gruenen thon Frauenlobs"
Berlin 24, f. 235, f. 483 (words only)
HM IV, 927

2. **Als Paulus die Jünger Christ versehret**
„Im vergessnen thon Frauenlobs"
Berlin 24, f. 244
HM IV, 930 ♪

3. **Auff ein Zeit gut Nachpauren sich**
„Im Blawen thon Frauenlobs"
Berlin 24, f. 241v; APSB 17

4. **Dem Son Gottes almechtig**
„Im Gailen thon Frauenlobs"
Berlin 24, f. 242v, 494 (words only); APSB 20

5. **Der kungynn ich ob allen kungyn dienen will**
„Im verholn don Frauenlobs"
Donaueschingen 257; Colmar 155; Berlin 24, f. 249r (no words)
Runge, Colmar 76 ♪

6. **Dez hymelz ercztenye**
„Dis ist Vrouwinlobis in dem wurgindrossil dy dry"
Wien 2701, f. 17; APSB 5
DTO XLI, 68 ♩

Do kuninc Alexander: *see* 8-29

7. **Ei ich sach in dem trone**
Colmar 19; München, Fragment M; Königsberg fragment; Wrocław I. Q. 368
„Diss ist unser frawen leich oder der guldin flügel zu latin Cantica Canticorum. Stent ie zwey lied in eym ton und in eym gemesse und sint der töne XXII der lieder XLIIII"
Runge, Colmar 3-16 ♪, facsimile 1; NOHM II, 258 ♩; ZfdA LXXXVI, 307-11 ♪
Record: History of Music in Sound, ii, side 11, Marienleich

– **Ein snider sneit mir min gewant**
„Aus unser Frouwen leich' Frauenlobs"
Wien 2701, f. 2
DTO XLI, 57 ♩

8. **Ein burger sass zu bretten**
„Im Würgendrüssel Frauenlobs"
Berlin 24, f. 228v
HM IV, 929 ¶

9. **Eyn ey gelich, ist synevel**
„In der froschwyse Frawenlobs"
Donauschingen 278; Colmar 136;
Berlin 24, f. 238v, 487 (no music);
APSB 15
Runge, Colmar 73 ¶
BMKH 291

– **Ein sneider sneit mir...**: *see* 8-7

10. **Ein wort, daz ist ein wesen**
„In Frawenlobes suessen ton"
Colmar 186; Berlin 24, f. 251 v
Runge, Colmar 88 ¶

11. **Ein wort daz wont ym allerhochsten trone**
„In Frauwenlobs gruntwys"
Colmar 194; Berlin 24, f. 246r,
497 (words only); APSB 23 ♩
Runge, Colmar 90 ¶

– **Ewiger, starcker, hoher, almechtiger Got**: *see* 35-6

12. **Fruchtenbernde frucht der welte trost**
„In Frauwenlobs leyt ton"
Donaueschingen 315; Colmar 188;
Berlin 24, f. 229v; APSB 8 ♩
Runge, Colmar 89 ¶

13. **Gar starc bekant ist der helfant**
„Im gecronten ton Frauenlops"
Donaueschingen 280; Colmar 157;
Berlin 24, f. 224v
Runge, Colmar 78 ¶

14. **Heyliger geist, herlucht min synne kamer**
„In Frauwenlobes überzarten don"
Donaueschingen 236; Colmar 28;
APSB 1 ♩
Runge, Colmar 16 ⌉
BMKH 188

15. **Herr... beschriben hat**
„In der Jar weiss Frauenlobs"
Berlin 24, 238r; APSB 14

16. **Her Symeon der wyse**
„In Frauwenlobes gruen don"
Donaueschingen 312; Colmar 212;
APSB 12 ♩
Runge, Colmar 102 ⌉

17. **Ich hoer' des vater lere jehen**
„Im zarten don"
Jena 110c; Berlin 24, f. 232r (no words), 242; APSB 6 ♩
HM IV, 830 ⌉, 927 ⌉; JHSB I, 190 ⌉, II, 68 ♩
HM III, 152

18. **Ich kam geritten uff ein felt**
„In Frauwenlobs dan ton"
Donauschingen 275; Colmar 128
Runge, Colmar 71 ⌉

19. **Ich mane dich, Gotes sun Jhesus, der tyfen wunden rot**
Wien 2701, f. 20
DTO XLI, 69 ♩
1 of 5 *Sprüche*

20. **Ich mane dich grozer note vumphe, muter, reyne mayt**
Wien 2701, f. 19
DTO XLI, 69 ♩
1 of 5 *Sprüche*

21. **Ich sach in einen garten gan**
„In der anckelwyse Frauwenlobs"
Colmar 241; Berlin 252r (no words)
Runge, Colmar 105 ♪; zfdA LXXX (1943), 98 ♩; GTM III, 14 ♩

– **Im andern Buch Samuelis**: 8-24

22. **Im geschicht schreiber Justino**
„In der Ritter Weiss Frauenlobs"
Berlin 24, f. 243r

23. **Im Mayen frü ein Jungling kun**
„Im Blüenden thon Frauenlobs"
Berlin 24, f. 240v; APSB 19 ♩

24. **In der Fasten kam zu ein dorff Pfaffen**
„Im geschwinden thon Frauenlobs"
Berlin 24, f. 236v; APSB 13 ♩

25. **In der offenbarung Johannes haben wir**
„Im langen thon Frauenlobs"
Berlin 24, f. 225v
HM IV, 926 ♪

26. **In einer weitbekanten stat**
„Im spätten thon Frauenlobs"
Berlin 24, f. 245r, 496 (words only); APSB 21

27. **In Gottes schoss gesehen wart in hoher art**
„Dyss ist Frauenlobs taugenhort oder sin slosshort"
Colmar 43
Runge, Colmar 28-49 ♪
BMKH 204
Frauenlob *or* Peter von Reichenbach? *See* BMKH 169, 181 *on authorship*

28. **Jacob der fuenfft ein kuenig in Schotlande**
„In der Zugweiss Frauenlobs"
Berlin 24, f. 239v; APSB 16
HM IV, 928 ♪

29. **Jesayas der schrybet so, der Gottes knecht**
„Im langen ton Frauwenlobes"
Donaueschingen 249; Colmar 94; APSB 4
Runge, Colmar 67 ♪
2nd stanza: Do kuninc Alexander myt vulkomner macht, JHSB II, 195 ♩

30. **Johannes der sach also fron**
„In Frauwenlobes spiegelwyse"
Colmar 163, 186; Berlin 24, f. 246v, 498 (words only); APSB 24
Runge, Colmar 82 ♪, 88 ♪

31. **Jung son und alter vater**
„In Frauwenlobs guldin tone"
Donaueschingen 255; Colmar 139; Berlin 24, f. 230; APSB 2 ♩
Runge, Colmar 74 ♪

32. **Karheit halber so hatte**
„Im Kupfer thon Frauenlobs"
Berlin 24, f. 234v, 481 (words only); APSB 11

33. **Klar thut Vicencius berichten**
„Im newen thon Frauenlobs"
Berlin 24, f. 227r; APSB 7
HM IV, 929 ♪

34. **Künig Wunibald in Burgund**
„In der Tagweiss Frauenlobs"
Berlin 24, f. 233r; APSB 9

35. **Lucas spricht klar**
„Gulden Radweise"
APSB 10 ♩

36. **Maria kunigynne**
„In der huntwyse Fr."
Donaueschingen 283; Colmar 161
Runge, Colmar 80, ♪ ; JHSB II, 196 ♩

37. **Maria, muter, reine meit**
„In Frauwenlobs Rytter wyse"
Donaueschingen 313; Colmar 222;
Berlin 24, f. 243r; APSB 18 ♩
Runge, Colmar 103 ♪

38. **Myn vroud ist gar czugangyn**
„In der grunen wyse"
Wien 2701, f. 17
DTO XLI, 67 ♩ ; SGMB 14 ♩
Spruch

39. **Nu geseygyn mich hut Got vater, sun und ouch heliger geyst**
Wien 2701, f. 19
DTO XLI, 68 ♩
Spruch

40. **Nu wil ich nymmermer vor zcwiln an dem hemilrich**
Wien 2701, f. 21
DTO XLI, 70 ♩
Spruch

41. **Nun aber war ein Brunnen daselbst an dem Ort**
„Der meisterliche Hort, in vier gekroenten Toenen... das ander Gesetz, im langen Ton Heinrichs Frauenlobs" (*Other* 3: 9-2, 25-9, 35-10)
APSB 3
HM IV, 933 ♪ ; Wagenseil 554 ♪

42. **O wip, du hoer eren haft**
„Das ist der mynnekliche leych"
Wien 2701, f. 34
DTO XLI, 77-83 ♩

43. **Richer man, Got lech dir gut, her hot dirs nicht gegebn**
Wien 2701, f. 22
DTO XLI, 70 ♩
Spruch

44. **Sint frolich, fraw, mit zuchten gein dem meyen**
„Her Frauwenlobs gecronter rey"
„In dem gecronten Rey weiss Frauenlobs"
Colmar 41; Donaueschingen 245; Berlin 24, f. 250r (no words)
Runge, Colmar 25 ♪
BMKH 201

45. **Sun, du bist sun, sun, ussertracht**
„Im zarten ton Frauwenlobs"
Donaueschingen 287; Colmar 196
Runge, Colmar 91 ♪
Wehrli 468

46. **Swa sich diu tugent erbiutet**
„Im vluk don"
Jena 106c
HM IV, 828 ♪; JHSB I, 184 ♪, II, 67 ♩
HM III, 141

47. **Us erentricher porten wart gesendet**
„In Frauenlobes zuegewyse"
Colmar 236
Runge, Colmar 104 ♪

48. **Usz alter ee schribet man uns besunder**
„Im vergessen ton Frauwenlobs *in antiquo dictamine*"
Colmar 166; Berlin 24, f. 244, 495 (words only); APSB 22
Runge, Colmar 82 ♪

49. **Von ainer edlen Frawen**
„In der Hagenblu weiss Frauenlobs"
Berlin 24, f. 247r; APSB 25

50. **Weil die Christen verfolget hart**
„Im Spiegelton Frauenlobs"
Berlin 24, f. 246
HM IV, 931 ♪

51. **Wer der trau Gott**
„In der gulden Radweiss Frauenlobs"
Berlin 24, f. 230v; APSB 10 ♩

52. **Wer hallff Adam uss not in fure**
„In dem nuwen ton Frauenlobs"
Donaueschingen 252; Colmar 176
Runge, Colmar 83 ♪

53. **Wer kante Gotes krefte**
„Im gruenen don"
Jena 108a; Wien 2701, f. 17a
HM IV, 829 ♪ ; JHSB I, 186 ♪, II, 68 ♩ ;
DTO XLI, 87 ♩
HM III, 144

54. **Wir leben hie in sunden**
„Im wurgendruessel Frauwenlobs"
Colmar 116
Runge, Colmar 70 ♪, XVII ♩

55. **Wo wundir werndir suz ursprink**
„Das ist des heylygyn cruecys leych"
Wien 2701, f. 22-23
DTO XLI, 71-77 ♩
Frauenlob or Regenbogen?
See 35-4

56. . . . .
„In der Hunds Fuss weiss Frauenlobs"
Berlin 24, f. 248r (no words)

57. . . . .
„Im Thon thon Frauenlobs"
Berlin 24,f. 251r (no words)

See also 36-6, 41-8

9. HEINRICH VON MÜGELN
1320?-1370?

TEBM 37; BMKH 180
Karl J. Schöer, *Die Dichtungen Heinrichs von Mügeln, nach den Hss. besprochen.* (Sitzungsberichte der Akademie der Wissenschaft zu Wien. Phil.-hist. Klasse, LV (1867), 451ff.). *Heinrichs von Mügeln kleineren Dichtungen* (Deutsche Texte des Mittelalters), 1959.

1. **Einen gecronten reyen**
„In meynster Heinrich von Mugelin traumton
Colmar 632; APSB 27 ♩
Runge, Colmar 140 ♪

2. **Genesis am neun und zwanzigstens uns bericht**
„Der meisterlich Hort, in vier gekroenten Toenen. Das erste Gesetz im langen Ton Heinrich Muglins" (*Other* 3: 8-41, 25-9, 35-10)
HM IV, 932 ♪; Wagenseil 554 ♪
See NOHM II, 259

3. **Hillf Herr Gott der Heyligen dein**
„Hoff ton"
APSB 29 ♩

4. **Wer nu der bybelbuch**
„Im kurtzenn Mueglins"
Colmar 611; APSB 30
Runge, Colmar 139 ♪

5. **Wer tichtet, und gesach nie warer kunste grunt**
„Hie volget meinster Heinrich von Mügelins gedichte, zuerst in sim langen tone."
„Heinrich Müglings langen ton. Ist der 4 gekroenten einer"
Colmar 592; Wien 2856; APSB 26
Runge, Colmar 137 ♪, 138 ♪

See 9-2

6. **Wilt du mentschart**
„In meinster Heinrich von Müglins grun ton"
Colmar 640; Wien 2856, f. 247; APSB 28 ♩
Runge, Colmar 140 𝄾

See 28

10. HEINRICH VON OFTERDINGEN
(Before 1250)

BMKH 158; TEBM 37: "a mythical figure"
A. Strack, *Zur Geschichte der Gedichte vom Wartburgkriege*. Diss. Berlin, 1883

1. **Das erste singen daz hie tut**
(Daz erste singen nu hie tuot)
„In dem gekauften oder in den fursten ton Heinrichs von Offertingen von erst die zwene kriege"
„Kreig von Wartburg"
„In des Düringe herren ton"
„In des edelen vursten dhon von Duryngelant..."
Colmar 756; Jena 123d
HM IV, 843 𝄾; Runge, Colmar, 165 𝄾;
JHSB I, 214 𝄾, II, 83 ♩, 199 ♩
HM II, I, 3

– HEINRICH DER TUGENDHAFTE SCHREIBER: 43 –

– DER HELLEVIUR: *see* HÖLLEFEUER –

11. DER HENNEBERGER

1. **Swer da gerne ritter wirt mit hoher wirdikeit**
Jena 36c
HM IV, 793 𝄾; JHSB I, 63 𝄾, II, 23 ♩
HM III, 39

12. HERMANN DER DAMEN

Helene Onnes, *De gedichten van Hermann der Damen*. Proefschr., Groningen, 1913

1. **Der aller wunder meister ist**
   Jena 118a
   HM IV, 839 𝄾 ; JHSB I, 205 𝄾 , II, 79 ♩
   HM III, 162

2. **Ein lop sing' ich dir ze prise**
   Jena 121b
   HM IV, 841 𝄾 ; JHSB I, 210 𝄾 , II, 81 ♩
   HM III, 167

3. **Het' ich al der werlde hulde**
   Jena 117d
   HM IV, 839 𝄾 ; JHSB I, 204 𝄾 , II, 79 ♩ ;
   GTM III, 13 ♩ ; Lang-Salmen 40 ♩
   HM III, 162

4. **Ich malc uf dcs sanges sims**
   Jena 122c
   HM IV, 841 𝄾 ; JHSB I, 212 𝄾 , II, 82 ♩
   HM III, 169

5. **In dirre wise ich singen wil**
   Jena 119b
   HM IV, 840 𝄾 ; JHSB I, 207 𝄾 , 80 ♩
   HM III, 164

6. **Ir Kristenen, alle schriet**
   Jena 113d-117d
   HM IV, 832-39 𝄾 ; JHSB I, 198 𝄾 , II, 71 ♩
   HM III, 160

13. HERMANN DER MÖNCH VON SALZBURG

XIV C

BMKH 184; Wehrli: „eigentlich zwei Hofdichtern"
F. A. Mayer und H. Rietsch, *Die Mondsee-Wiener Liederhandschrift und der Mönch von Salzburg*, *Acta Germanica* III, 4-IV. Berlin, 1894-96.

1. **Ave, Balsams creatur**
„Des Munchs von Salczburg guldin abc"
Colmar 653; München, Cgm. 715, f. 46; Wien 2856, f. 166
Runge, Colmar, 145-150 ♪
HM III, 468

2. **Beschnytten wirdiclichen**
„Des Munches *Cisiojanus* die jarwyse"
Colmar 662
Runge, Colmar, 154 ♪ ; GFML 194 ♩

3. **Die nacht wirt schier des hymmels gast**
„Dyss ist des Munchs korwyse"
Colmar 658; Berlin 25, p. 31; APSB 87
Runge, Colmar, 153 ♪

4. **Gar lys, in senfter wys**
„Dyss ist daz taghorn dez Munchs von Salzpurg"
Colmar 657; Wien 2856, f. 186
Runge, Colmar, 150 ♪ ; G. Adler, *Vierteljahrschrift für Musikwissenschaft* II (1886), 310-12 ♪, ♩ ; GMMA 225 ♩

5. **Her Got almechtig, dry person**
„Darnach manche von Salzburg des Munchs zarter don"
Colmar 644; München, Cgm. 715, f. 715; Wien 2856, f. 178; Berlin 24, f. 158 (no words)
Runge, Colmar, 141 ♪

6. **Ich bit dich, geber guter dinge**
„In des Muenchs suessen ton. etlich sprechen korwyse"
Colmar 652
Runge, Colmar, 144 ♪

7. **Kum senfter trost, heiliger geist**
„Im Munch von Salczburg langen tone"
Colmar 646; Donaueschingen 222; Wien 2856, f. 182; München, Cgm. 715, f. 162; APSB 88 ♩
Runge, Colmar, 142 ♪

8. **Magt hochgeborn von dem geslecht Jesse**
„In des Munches hoffdone"
Colmar 645; München, Cgm. 715, ff. 175, 177; Wien 2856, f. 242; Berlin 24, f. 160 (no words)
Runge, Colmar, 142 ♪

9. **Maria, wyss gegrüsset!**
„In des Munchs von Salczburgk kurzen ton"
Colmar 661; Berlin 24, f. 161 (no words)
Runge, Colmar, 153 ♪

10. **Mein traut gesell, mein liebster hort**
MGDM I, 180 ♩
O. Ursprung, AfMW IV (1922), 413 ♪, ♩

11. **Mucs ich mich von dir schaiden**
AfMW V (1923), 29 ♩

12. **Myn liebste fraw, in lieber acht**
„Das nachthorn"
Colmar 658; Wien 2856, ff. 185, 245
Runge, Colmar, 152 ♪; Adler, *op. cit.* 4, *supra*, 312-315 ♪, ♩

13. **Wol mich wart! ain frëwelein czart**
AfMW V (1923), 29 ♩

14. DER HÖLLEFEUER
2/2 XIII C

1. **In diser wise daz erste liet**
Jena 30a
HM IV, 791 ♪; JHSB I, 56 ♪, II, 20 ♩
HM III, 33

15. HUGO (VIII, GRAF) VON MONTFORT
1375-1423

Paul Runge, *Die Lieder des Hugo von Montfort mit den Melodien des Burk Mangolt.* Leipzig, Breitkopf und Härtel, 1906. Pp. 75. (Texts, original notation, modern transcription, 1 facsimile).
J. E. Wackernell, *Hugo von Montfort.* 1881.
Karl Bartsch, *Hugo von Montfort* (Bibl. Litt. Verein Stuttgart, CXLIII), Tübingen, 1879.
E. Jammers, „Die Melodien Hugos von Montfort", AfMw XIII (1956), 217-35.
MS: Heidelberg, Univ. Bibl., Cod. Pal. germ. 329 (folios given below).

„Die weysen hat gemachen
Bürk Mangolt
Unser getrewer knecht."
Hugo von Montfort

1. **Des hiemels vogt und hochster keiser**
f. 50
Runge, 65 ¶, 68 ♩
Bartsch: „Unecht", *but see* Runge 4

2. **Fraw wilt du wissen was es ist**
f. 21v
Runge, 42 ¶, 43 ♩ ; Wolf, *Handbuch der Notationskunde*, I, 177-78 ♩, facsimile

3. **Fro welt ir sint gar hüpsch und schön**
f. 35r
Runge, 45 ¶, 46 ♩, facsimile, frontispiece
MGDM I, 190 ♩

4. **Ich fragt ein wachter ob es wer tag**
f. 11r
Runge, 26 ¶, 27 ♩
Wehrli, 332

5. **Ich fröw mich gen des absentz kunst**
f. 10v
Runge, 23 ¶, 23 ♩

6. **Ich var uff wag des bittern mer**
f. 13r
Runge, 37 ¶, 38 ♩

7. **Könd ich ein gedicht volbringen**
f. 48v
Runge, 57 ♪, 59 ♩
Bartsch: „Unecht", *but see* Runge 4

8. **Mich straft ein wachter des morgens frü**
f. 11v
Runge, 29 ♪, 31 ♩

9. **Sag an wachter wie was es tag**
f. 12v
Runge, 34 ♪, 35 ♩

10. **Weka wekh die zarten lieben**
f. 46r
Runge, 20 ♩, 52 ♪, 54 ♩

16. DER KANZLER
Fl. 1300

TEBM 32; BMKH 167
H. Krieger, *Der Kanzler. Ein mhd. Spruch- und Liederdichter um 1300.* Diss. Bonn, 1931

1. **Am zwei und viertzigisten beschreibt Esaias fein**
„Im gulden Ton Cantzlers"
Berlin 25, p. 14
HM IV, 925 ♪

2. **David, din blick sint worden war**
„Item in Kanczlers langen tone"
Colmar 552
Runge, Colmar, 134 ♪

3. **Frou Minne, getiuret si din nam**
„In des Kanczlers sussen done"
Colmar 554
Runge, Colmar, 135 ♪
HM III, 454; KLD I, 215

4. **Got schepher aller dingen**
Stanza 12: Was wird und hôher êre
„In des Kanczlers hohen gulden tone"
Colmar 545; APSB 62
Runge, Colmar, 130 𝅘𝅥𝅮
KLD I, 187; BMKH 486
Stanza 15: Jôhannes in dem trône
sach Got in sîner majestât
„In dysem hohen guldin Canczler..."
KLD I, 187; BMKH 488

5. **Ich weiss ein keyserliche meyt**
„In des Kanczlers hofdone"
Colmar 553; Berlin 24, f. 157v
(no words)
Runge, Colmar, 135 𝅘𝅥𝅮 HM IV, 931 𝅘𝅥𝅮
BMKH 55

– **Johannes in dem trône...**: 16-4

– **Was wird und hoher ere**: 16-4

17. MEISTER KELIN
2/2 XIII C

1. **Ein künik in sime troume sach**
Jena 16c
HM IV, 780 𝅘𝅥𝅮; JHSB I, 31 𝅘𝅥𝅮, II, 8 𝅘𝅥
HM III, 20

2. **Ez ist vil maniger here**
Jena 18b; Basel, N.J. 3, nr. 145
HM IV, 781 𝅘𝅥𝅮; JHSB I, 34 𝅘𝅥𝅮, II, 10 𝅘𝅥
HM III, 22; JHSB II, 154, *re* Basel fragment

3. **Vil riche saelde, mich nimt immer wunder**
Jena 17c; Basel N.J. 3, nr. 145
HM IV, 781 𝅘𝅥𝅮; JHSB I, 33 𝅘𝅥𝅮, II, 9 𝅘𝅥
HM III, 21

18. KLINGSOR

XIII C

BMKH 158; TEBM 39: „a mythical figure"

1. **Ein edelbaum gewachsen ist**
   „In Clingesores swarczen ton"
   Colmar 680; Jena 134c (text only);
   APSB 59 („Klinges Uhr")
   Runge, Colmar, 159 ♪; JHSB II, 198 ♩
   HM III, 181, „Kriek von Wartberk"

19. KONRAD VON QUEINFURT

– 1382

1. **Du lenze gut, des jares tiurste quarte**
   Leipzig, Univ. Bibl., ms. 1305, ff. 107-110
   MGDM I, 177 ♩

20. KONRAD VON WÜRZBURG

1225?-1287

BMKH 164
Konrad von Würzburg, *Partonopier und Meliur... Lieder und Sprüche*, hrsg. von Karl Bartsch. Wien, 1871
E. Schröder, *Konrads von Würzburg kleinere Dichtungen*, III. Berlin, Weidmann, 1959.

1. **Auss der dieffe schrei ich zu dir**
   „Im abgespitzten Ton Conr. von Wirtzburg"
   Berlin 25, p. 23; APSB 64
   HM IV, 924 ♪

2. **Ave, ich lobe dich, reine meit**
   „In Cunrads von Wirczburg nachtwyse. *Alii dicunt esse* In Frider. von Suneburg sussem don"
   Colmar 526
   Runge, Colmar, 127 ♪

3. **Ave Maria, kusche maget stete**
   „In Cunradz von Wirczburg morgenwyse"
   Colmar 512
   Runge, Colmar, 126 ♪

4. **Der nit sin vaz vil tunkel verwet, als ein bleich gehilwe**
   Jena 101b
   HM IV, 827 ♪ ; JHSB I, 168 ♪, II, 66 ♩

5. **Dez soltu clein geniessen**
   „In Conratz von Wirtzburg kurczen oder im werden don"
   Colmar 528
   Runge, Colmar, 128 ♪ ; GTM III, 9 ♩
   BMKH 465

6. **Er mag vil lichte witze han**
   „In meinster Cunratz von Wirczeburg blawen ton"
   Colmar 541; APSB 45, ascribed to „Bartel Regenbogen, des Schmides"
   Runge, Colmar, 129 ♪
   BMKH 484

7. **Hochvart ist worden also gross**
   „In meinster Cunrades von Wirczburg auspis"
   Colmar 506
   Runge, Colmar, 126 ♪
   BMKH 456

8. **Waz in dem paradys ie wart gebildet und gemachet**
   „In Cunrads von Wirczburg hoff don"
   Colmar 531; APSB 63
   Runge, Colmar, 128 ♪
   BMKH 467

9. **Woluff ir geist, hin uber mer**
   „Meinster Cunrads guldin reyel"
   Colmar 43
   Runge, Colmar, 27 ♪

– KRIEG VON WARBURG: *see* 10-1; 18-1; 56-1 –

21. LESCH
XV-XVI C

BMKH 184; TEBM 39
L. Köster, *Albrecht Lesch* (*Ein Münchener Meistersänger d. 16 Jhs.*)
Diss. München, 1937

1. **Ave Maria, dich lobet musica**
   „Diss ist Leschen guldyner reye"
   Donaueschingen 219; Colmar 37
   Runge, Colmar, 21 ♪

2. **Daz recht ist manigfeltig krump**
   „Dyss ist in Leschen hoffwyse"
   Colmar 837
   Runge, Colmar, 179 ♪

3. **Gott herr, din ewikeite**
   „Leschen getichte. Sin cirkelwyse"
   Colmar 831; APSB 73 ♩; Berlin 25, p.38
   (no words)
   Runge, Colmar, 177 ♪

4. **Ich lob die reinen frauwen zart**
   „In Leschen fur wyse"
   Colmar 835; Berlin 25, p. 36 (no
   words); APSB 72 („Feuerw.")
   Runge, Colmar, 178 ♪
   BMKH 84

5. **Wer nympt mit lieb das hochste gut**
   „Leschen sang wyse"
   Colmar 839; APSB 71
   Runge, Colmar, 180 ♪

6. **Zuch durch die wolken, myn gesang**
   „Leschen tagwyse"
   Colmar 843
   Runge, Colmar, 181 ♪
   BMKH 87

22. LIEBE VON GIENGEN
XIV C

BMKH 183

1. **O Maria, du reine meit**
   „Ein anders sinem senften ton"
   Colmar 792
   Runge, Colmar, 170 ♪
   BMKH 79

2. **Was sol ein meder uff daz mat**
„In des Lieben jarwyse"
Colmar 790; APSB 91
Runge, Colmar, 169 ♪

3. . . . . *blurred*
„In der Radweis Lieben von Gengen"
Berlin 25, p. 40

23. DER LITSCHAUER

1. **Man sach hie voren die alten herren eren pflegen**
Jena 42a
HM IV, 796 ♪; JHSB I, 73 ♪, II, 26 ♩
HM III, 46

24. MAGISTER HUIUS LIBRI (SC. COLMAR)

BMKH 186

1. **Ich singe gerne lyse**
„Im unerkanten ton. V Liedt..."
Colmar 492; Donaueschingen 212; APSB 93, ascribed to „Wolf Nestler von Ulm"
Runge, Colmar, 123 ♪

25. DER MARNER
Fl. 1230-1244

TEBM 40; BMKH 160
Philip Strauch, *Der Marner*. Strassburg, Trübner, 1876 (Quellen und Forschungen, XIV)

1. **Das auf Erd nicht schedlicher sag**
„Im Kreutz thon Marners"
Berlin 24, f. 256r; APSB 32 ♩

2. **Esaias der Prophet spricht**
„Im suessen thon Marners"
Berlin 24, f. 259r (no words); APSB 34 ♩

3. **Ich lob ein meit ubr alle lant**
„Der propheten dantz ein eygen getticht des Marners"
Colmar 489; Berlin 24, f. 252v; APSB 36
Runge, Colmar 121 ♪
BMKH 47-49; Strauch 63

4. **Ich mercke, daz diu sonne**
„In Marners kurczem oder hofedone"
Colmar 494; Berlin 24, f. 257r; APSB 33
Runge, Colmar 125 ♪
BMKH 444; Strauch 130, *as* „Anhang" *to* Marner's Ob allen frouwen frouwe; Strauch 60-61

5. **Im heiligen Matheo klar**
„Im langen thon Marners"
Berlin 24, f. 254v
HM IV, 923 ♪
See 25-8

6. **In ein fuerneme stat hinkam**
„Im gulden thon Marners"
Berlin 24, f. 258r; APSB 35 ♩
HM IV, 923 ♪
Strauch 59

7. **Ir schauwent an die clein ameiss**
„Dyss par stet in Marners tone"
Colmar 490
Runge, Colmar 122 ♪
BMKH 442

8. **Maria, muter, reine meit**
„Dyss ist des Marners lange ton"
„Im langen Marner ton. Ist der 4 gekroenten thone einer"
Colmar 447; APSB 31
Runge, Colmar 119 ♪, 120 ♩
Strauch 61-63
See 25-5, 25-9

9. **Nach den aber das werk verricht**
„Der meisterliche Hort, in vier gekroenten tonen... Das dritte Gesetz, im langen ton Ludwig Marners" (*Other* 3:8-41, 9-2, 35-10)
HM IV, 934 ¶; Wagenseil 554 ¶
See 25-5, 25-8

26. MEFFRID

XIV C

BMKH 181

1. **Hercz unde synn, nu muewe dich**
„Meinster Meffryds geticht"
Colmar 794; Engelberg
Runge, Colmar, 171 ¶; *Schweizer Jahrbuch f.M.W.*, 1928, p. 64f.; *Kirchenmusik Jahrbuch* XXI (1908), 49
BMKH 550

27. MEISSNER

2/2 XIII C

A. Frisch, *Untersuchungen über die verschiedenen mhd. Dichter, welche nach der Ueberlieferung den Namen Meissner führen.* Diss. Jena, 1887

1. **Almehtik Got, barmunge rich, sich hie nider in diz elende**
Jena 94a
HM IV, 824 ¶; JHSB I, 157 ¶, II, 62 ♩
HM III, 102

2. **Daz sank daz hoeste si in himele unde uf erden**
Jena 91d
HM IV, 823 ¶; JHSB I, 153 ¶, II, 60 ♩
HM III, 99

3. **Got, aller saelden ane vank, dir si genigen**
Jena 81a
HM IV, 817 ¶; JHSB I, 135 ¶, II, 53 ♩
HM III, 86

4. **Got, der ging durch uns einer jemerlichen gang**
„Der Michsener in sim gedicht"
Colmar 797
Runge, Colmar, 171 ♪

5. **Got der hat uns nach im gebildet**
Jena 94d
HM IV, 825 ♪ ; JHSB I, 158 ♪, II, 62 ♩
HM III, 103

6. **Got ist gewaltik**
Jena 87b
HM IV, 820 ♪ ; JHSB I, 146 ♪, II, 56 ♩ ;
Riemann 269 ♩
HM III, 94

7. **...hat / sin hant getat** (*incomplete*)
Jena 86a
HM IV, 819 ♪ ; JHSB I, 144 ♪, II, 55 ♩
HM III, 92

8. **Ich wiste gerne, wa bi man die ritter solte erkennen, ich sie vil...** (*incomplete*)
Jena 92d
HM IV, 824 ♪ ; JHSB I, 155 ♪, II, 61 ♩
HM III, 100

9. **Kün' ich nu undersheiden wol zwene namen, wib und vrouwe, des wolt' ich mich vlizen**
Jena 97a
HM IV, 826 ♪ ; JHSB I, 162 ♪, II, 64 ♩
HM III, 105

10. **Maria, muoter, meit und Kristes amme**
Jena 83a
HM IV, 818 ♪ ; JHSB I, 139 ♪, II, 53 ♩
HM III, 88

11. **Mich wundert, wie die wolken vliegen tak und naht**
Jena 88b
HM IV, 820 ♪ ; JHSB I, 148 ♪, II, 57 ♩
HM III, 95

12. **Sündige lust ist also sueze**
Jena 95d
HM IV, 826 ♪ ; JHSB I, 160 ♪, II, 63 ♩
HM III, 103

13. **Swelich man ein werrer wesen wil**
Jena 93c
HM IV, 824 ♪ ; JHSB I, 156 ♪, II, 61 ♩ ;
zfdA LXXX (1943-44), 95 ♩
HM III, 101

14. **Vil sueze zarte minne**
Jena 85c
HM IV, 819 ♪ ; JHSB I, 143 ♪, II, 54 ♩
HM III, 91

15. **Vlize dich, mensche, an guotin wort**
Jena 91c
HM IV, 822 ♪ ; JHSB I, 153 ♪, II, 60 ♩
HM III, 99

16. **Vür alliu wunder, diu nu sint, merket ein michel wunder**
Jena 89d
HM IV, 821 ♪ ; JHSB I, 150 ♪, II, 58 ♩
HM III, 97

17. **Zwiveler an deme gelouben, sich an Gotes wunder**
Jena 90c
HM IV, 822 ♪ ; JHSB I, 151 ♪, II, 59 ♩
HM III, 98

– MÖNCH VON SALZBURG: *see* HERMANN DER MÖNCH –

28. MÜLICH VON PRAG

XIV C

TEBM 40; BMKH 179
R. Batka, *Die Lieder Mulichs von Prag*. 1905

1. **Got, dine wunder manigfalt**
   „In Mülichs von Prage langer tone"
   Colmar 781
   Runge, Colmar, 168 ⌝

2. **Nu siht man aber beide**
   „Mülichs von Prage rey"
   Colmar 40
   Runge, Colmar, 24 ⌝
   Lang-Salmen 58 ♩, 19, facsimile
   BMKH 199

See 9-3: *Ascription to* Mülich von Prag *in* APSB 29

29. MUSCATBLUT
-1439?

BMKH 185
E. v. Groote, *Die Lieder Muskatbluts*. Köln, 1852.

1. **Dung hab, der an begynne**
   „Muscatbl. nuwer ton"
   Colmar 74; APSB 83 ♩
   Runge, Colmar, 65 ⌝

2. **Esechiel der Prophet hel**
   „Hoffton"
   APSB 84 ♩

3. **Got vatter worcht on alle vorcht**
   „Muscatblutz alter ton"
   Colmar 79
   Runge, Colmar, 66 ⌝

30. NEIDHART VON REUENTHAL
1190?-1246?

Moriz Haupt und E. Wiessner, *Neidharts Lieder*. Leipzig, 1923.
K. Ameln und W. Rössle, *Tanzlieder Neidharts von Reuenthal*. Jena, 1927.
Friedrich Gennrich, *Melodien altdeutscher Lieder. 47 Melodien in handschriftlicher Fassung*. Darmstadt, Musikwissenschaftliche Studienbibliothek, Heft 9, 1954.
Edmund Wiessner, *Kommentar zu Neidharts Liedern*. Leipzig, Hirzel, 1954.
Lieder von Neidhart (von Reuental), bearbeitet von Wolfgang

Schmieder; Revision des Textes von Edmund Wiessner. Mit Reproduction der Handschriften. Wien, Universal, 1930 (Denkmäler der Tonkunst in Österreich, LXXI) (abbrev.: DTO).
A. T. Hatto, R. J. Taylor, *The Songs of Neidhart von Reuental. 17 Summer and winter songs, set to their original melodies, with translations and a musical and metrical cannon.* Manchester, University Press, 1958. (abbrev.: HT).
F. Keinz, *Neidharts von Reuenthals Lieder.* 1910
E. Wiessner, *Die Lieder Neidharts.* Tübingen, Niemeyer, 1955. Texts included in this edition starred below.
See also Berlin 779. HM *pages not given, since* DTO LXXI *replaces this edition.*

*1. **Allez, daz den sumer her mit vreuden was**
Berlin 779, f. 215
DTO LXXI, 36 ♩ ; HT 42 ♩
Wehrli 348

*2. **Blôzen wir den anger ligen sâhen**
Berlin 779, f. 159
DTO LXXI, 33 ♩ ; HT 14 ♩

3. **Der mey der chumpt mit reicher wat**
Vipiteno f. 49
DTO LXXI, 40 ♩
„Pseudo-Neidhart"

4. **Der may gar wunnecleichen hat**
Vipiteno f. 51
DTO LXXI, 40 ♩
„Pseudo-Neidhart"

5. **Der may hat menig hercze hoch erstaigett**
Berlin 779, f. 160
DTO LXXI, 33 ♩ ; DAHA I, 18 ♩
„Pseudo-Neidhart"

6. **Der sumer kumpt mit reichem geuden**
Berlin 779, f. 201
DTO LXXI, 35 ♩
„Pseudo-Neidhart"

7. **Der sumer kumpt mit reicher watt**
Berlin 779, f. 198
DTO LXXI, 35 ♩
„Pseudo-Neidhart"

8. **Der sunnen (sumer) glast wenns von dem hymel scheynet**
Berlin 779, f. 163; Wien 3344, f. 107
DTO LXXI, 33 ♩; Gennrich, *Melodien altd. Lieder*, 11 ♪
„Pseudo-Neidhart"

9. **Der swarcze dorn ist worden weis**
Berlin 779, f. 131; Wien 3344, f. 105
DTO LXXI, 31 ♩; Gennrich, *Melodien altd. Lieder*, 8 ♪
„Pseudo-Neidhart"

10. **Der vil lieben sumerzeit**
Berlin 779, f. 171; Wien 3344, f. 106
DTO LXXI, 34 ♩
„Pseudo-Neidhart"

11. **Der winter hat mit siben sachen uns verjagt**
Berlin 779, f. 267
DTO LXXI, 39 ♩; Gennrich, *Melodien altd. Lieder*, 10 ♪
„Pseudo-Neidhart"

*12. **Des sumers und des winders beider veintschaft**
Berlin 779, f. 217
DTO LXXI, 36 ♩; HT 44 ♩

13. **Die liechten tag beginnen aber trüben**
Berlin 779, f. 260
DTO LXXI, 39 ♩
„Pseudo-Neidhart"

*14. **Do der liebe summer**
Berlin 779, f. 228
DTO LXXI, 37 ♩; Gennrich, *Melodien altd. Lieder*, 3 ♪; HT 20 ♩

15. **Do man den gumpel gampel sank**
Wien 3344, f. 107
DTO LXXI, 40 ♩; Gennrich, *Melodien altd. Lieder*, 1 ♪
„Pseudo-Neidhart"

*16. **Ez gruonet wol diu heide**
München, Staatsbibliothek, Cod. lat. 4660 (Carmina Burana)
Neidhart *melody accompanying* „Annualis mea"?

17. **Freut euch wolgemuten kindt**
Berlin 779, f. 152; Wien 3344, f. 108
DTO LXXI, 32 ♩
„Pseudo-Neidhart"

18. **Ich claghe de blomen und de wunnenlichen zit**
Frankfurt f. 4
DTO LXXI, 42 ♩

19. **Ich musz aber clagen gar von schulden**
Berlin 779, f. 250
DTO LXXI, 38 ♩
„Pseudo-Neidhart"

20. **Ich wen einen zagen**
Berlin 779, f. 200
DTO LXXI, 35 ♩ ; Gennrich, *Melodien altd. Lieder* 7 ⌉
„Pseudo-Neidhart"

*21. **Ine gesach die heide**
(Ich sah die haide)
Berlin 779, f. 153
DTO LXXI, 33 ♩ ; GTM III, 7a ♩ ; GFML 239 ♩ ; Ameln-Rössle 6; Gennrich, *Melodien altd. Lieder* 2 ⌉, *Mhd. Liedkunst* 19 ⌉ ; HT 12 ♩

22. **Ir schawet an den lenczen gut**
Berlin 779, f. 164
DTO LXXI, 34 ♩
„Pseudo-Neidhart"

23. **Kinder ir habt einen wintter an der handt**
Berlin 779, f. 224
DTO LXXI, 37 ♩
„Pseudo-Neidhart"

*24. **Kint, bereitet iuch der sliten ûf daz îs!**
Berlin 779, f. 236
DTO LXXI, 37 ♩; MGDM I, 166 ♩; Gennrich, *Melodien altd. Lieder* 2 ♪;
HT 16 ♩; GMMA 228 ♩

25. **Mann hort nicht mer süssen schal**
Berlin 779, f. 255
DTO LXXI, 39 ♩
„Pseudo-Neidhart"

26. **May hat wunniglich entsprossen**
Berlin 779, f. 136
DTO LXXI, 31 ♩; GFML 225 ♩;
GMMA 227 ♩; Gennrich, *Melodien altd. Lieder* 12 ♪; Riemann 365 ♩
„Pseudo-Neidhart"

27. **Mayenzeit one neidt**
Berlin 779, f. 149
DTO LXXI, 32 ♩; GTM III, 7C ♩;
GMMA 227 ♩; HGEM 21 ♩;
Gennrich, *Melodien altd. Lieder* 12 ♪;
Riemann 266 ♩
„Pseudo-Neidhart"

28. **Meie, din liehter schin**
Vipiteno f. 53
DTO LXXI, 41 ♩

29. **Mey, du wunnenbernde zyt**
Colmar 69
„Dyss ist h' Nytharcz ffrass"
Runge, Colmar, 62 ♪, XVIII ♩;
DTO LXXI, 42 ♩
See 30-30

30. **Meye dein wunnewerde zeit**
Vipiteno f. 59
DTO LXXI, 41 ♩
„Pseudo-Neidhart"

31. **Mir is ummaten leyde**
Frankfurt f. 1
DTO LXXI, 41 ♩

*32. **Mir ist von herzen leide**
Frankfurt f. 1; Berlin 779, f. 219
HM IV, 770, facsimile; DTO LXXI, 36 ♩; Gennrich, *Melodien altd. Lieder* 4 ˥; HT 34 ♩

33. **Nyemant soll sein trawren tragen lennger**
Berlin 779, f. 178; Wien 3344, f. 104
DTO LXXI, 35 ♩
„Pseudo-Neidhart"

34. **Niu horent wie sie all gemayne tihtent!**
Vipiteno f. 57
DTO LXXI, 41 ♩ (*incomplete*)

*35. **Nu klag' ich die bluomen und die liehten sumerzît**
Berlin 779, f. 256
DTO LXXI, 39 ♩; HT 28 ♩

36. **Nun hat maye wunniglich beschonett**
Berlin 779, f. 147r-v
DTO LXXI, 32 ♩

– **Nu var hin, vil ungedaner winter**
See 30-34
Incipit of text of 30-34

*37. **Owê dirre nôt!**
Berlin 779, f. 220
DTO LXXI, 36 ♩; GFML 229 ♩; Gennrich,
Melodien altd. Lieder 2 ˥, *Mhd. Liedkunst* 20 ˥; HT 38 ♩

*38. **Owê dirre sumerzît**
Berlin 779, f. 240
DTO LXXI, 38 ♩; Gennrich, *Melodien altd. Lieder* 6 ˥; HT 24 ♩

*39. **Owê, lieber sumer, dîner liehten tage lange**
Berlin 779, f. 238
DTO LXXI, 38 ♩ ; HT 22 ♩

– **Owê liebe sumerzeit**
See 30-38

*40. **Owê summerzît**
Berlin 779, f 222; Wien 3344, f. 106
DTO LXXI, 36 ♩ ; HT 32 ♩

41. **Owe winter, wie du hast beczwungen**
Berlin 779, f. 258
DTO LXXI, 39 ♩
„Pseudo-Neidhart"

42. **Seytt die lieben summertage**
Berlin 779, f. 214
DTO LXXI, 35 ♩ ; Gennrich, *Melodien altd. Lieder* 9 ⌉
„Pseudo-Neidhart"

*43. **Si klagent, daz der winder**
Berlin 779, f. 213
DTO LXXI, 35 ♩ ; Gennrich, *Melodien altd. Lieder* 7 ♩ ; HT 40 ♩

*44. **Sinc an, guldîn huon! ich gibe dir weize**
Berlin 779, f. 234; Frankfurt f. 3
DTO LXXI, 37 ♩, 42 ♩ ; GTM III, 7b ♩ ; MGDM I, 165 ♩ ; Gennrich, *Melodien altd. Lieder* 4 ⌉, *Mhd. Liedkunst* 18 ⌉; HT 18-19 ♩
Ameln-Rössle 16; Wehrli 342

*45. **Sumer, dîner süezen weter müezen wir uns ânen**
Vipiteno f. 52
DTO LXXI, 40 ♩ ; HT 30 ♩

*46. **Sumer unde winder**
Frankfurt f. 1
DTO LXXI, 41 ♩ ; HM IV, 770, facsimile;
HT 26 ♩

– **Sumers und des winders beider vientschaft:** *see* 30-12

47. **Tochter spynn den rocken**
Berlin 779, f. 168
DTO LXXI, 34 ♩

48. **Uns ist komen ein liebe zeit**
Vipiteno f. 48
DTO LXXI, 40 ♩
„Pseudo-Neidhart"

49. **Urlaub hab der winter**
Berlin 779, f. 148; Vipiteno f. 47
DTO LXXI, 32 ♩, 40 ♩
„Pseudo-Neidhart"

50. **Was mir sender swäre**
Berlin 779, f. 253
DTO LXXI, 38 ♩
„Pseudo-Neidhart"

– **Wie schön wir den anger ligen sâhen**
See 30-2

– **Willekome eyn som... suze**
Frankfurt, f. 2
DTO LXXI, 42 ♩
See 30-52

51. **Willekomen mayenschein**
Berlin 779, f. 141
DTO LXXI, 31 ♩ ; Parrish and Ohl, *Musical Masterpieces*, 13 ♩ ; Riemann 264 ♩
„Pseudo-Neidhart"

52. **Willekomen, sumerweter süeze**
Frankfurt f. 2
DTO LXXI, 42 ♩

– Winder...: *see* Winter...

53. **Winter deine zeit**
Berlin 779, f. 137
DTO LXXI, 31 ♩
„Pseudo-Neidhart"

54. **Winter deiner kunfft der trawret sere**
Berlin 779, f. 252
DTO LXXI, 38 ♩
„Pseudo-Neidhart"

*55. **Winder, dîniu meil**
Berlin 779, f. 231
DTO LXXI, 37 ♩ ; HT 36 ♩

56. **Winter dir zu laide**
Berlin 779, f. 166-67
DTO LXXI, 34 ♩ ; Gennrich, *Melodien altd. Lieder* 9 ♪
„Pseudo-Neidhart"

57. **Winder wie ist nu dein kraft**
Berlin 779, f. 142
DTO LXXI, 32 ♩ ; NOHM II, 256 ♩ ; DAHA I, 19 ♩ ; Gennrich, *Melodien altd. Lieder* 10 ♪; Riemann 265 ♩
„Pseudo-Neidhart"

– **Wis willkomen meienshin**: 51

58. **Wol dir liebe sumerzeit**
Berlin 779, f. 134
DTO LXXI, 31 ♩
„Pseudo-Neidhart"

59. **Wol geczieret stet der plan**
Berlin 779, f. 176; Wien 3344, f. 104
DTO LXXI, 34 ♩
„Pseudo-Neidhart"

60. **Wolt ir hörn ein news geschiht**
Vipiteno f. 54
DTO LXXI, 41 ♩

31. OSWALD VON WOLKENSTEIN

1377?-1430?

Oswald von Wolkenstein, *Geistliche und weltliche Lieder bearbeitet, der Text von Josef Schatz, die Musik von Oswald Koller.* DTO XVIII (Jg. IX[1]) Wien, Artaria & Co, 1902. XXII, 233 pp. Single voice, nos. 1-83; polyphonic, 84-116; Entwürfe und unvollständiges, 117-24, * *below;* T *marks texts,* pp. 14-84.

Mss: A. Wien 2777. 37 × 27 cm. 61ff. XV C.
B. Innsbruck, Universitätsbibliothek. 49 × 34 cm. 48ff. XV C.
C. Innsbruck, Museum Ferdinandeum, IV, C.I. 21 × 15 cm. 115ff. Paper. XV C. No music.
D. London, British Museum, Add. 24,946. 85 ff. XV C. No music.

1. **Ach Got, wär ich ein pilgerein**
B 38
DTO 139 𝄾, 23 T

2. **Ach senleiches leiden**
A 20, B 23
DTO 177 ♩, 21 T

3. **Ain anevank an götlich vorcht**
A 1, B 1
DTO 139 𝄾, 140 𝄾, 51 T

*4. **Ain ellend schid durch zahers flins**
A 37
DTO 206 𝄾, 23 T

*5. **Ain erens schatz an tadels ort**
A 37
DTO 206 𝄾, 23 T

6. **Ain graserin durch kuelen tau**
A 36, B 36
DTO 177 ♩, 221 𝄾, 32 T

7. **Ain guet geporen edelman**
A 47, B 19 DTO 178 ♩, 179 𝄾, 22T, facsimile, frontispiece

8. **Ain jeterin, junk, frisch, frei, fruet**
A 43, B 34, B 37
DTO 140 𝄾, 141 𝄾, 32 T

9. **Ain mensch von achzen jaren klueg**
A 8, B 26
DTO 141 ♪, 14 T

– **Ain purger und ain hofman**
DTO 69 T
Melody of 31-16

10. **Ain rainklich weib durch jugent schön**
A 40, B 34
DTO 141 ♪, 142 ♪, 43 T

11. **Ain tunkle varb in occident**
A 30, B 16
DTO 142 ♪, 45 T

12. **a. Ave mueter, fraue, magt und maid**
b. Ave mueter küniginne
B 44
DTO 205 ♩, 82 T

13. **Bog depre mi was duster da**
A 15
DTO 143 ♪, 23 T

– **Der himelfürst mich heut bewar**
DTO 63 T
Melody of 31-59

14. **Der mai mit lieber zal**
A 19, B 22
DTO 179 ♩, 31 T; DAHA 64 ♩; J. Wolf, *Geschichte der Mensuralnotation* II, 140 ♪, III, 186 ♩; ZfdA LXXXII, 120 ♩

– **Der oben swebt und niden hebt**
DTO 54 T
Melody of 31-59

15. **Der seines laids ergetet well sein**
A 33
DTO 143 ♪, 37 T

16. **Des grossen herren wunder**
A 29, B 11
DTO 143 ♪, 47 T

17. **Des himmels trone empfärbet sich**
A 34, B 16
DTO 182 ♩, ♪, 223 ♪, 26 T

18. **Die minne füeget niemand**
A 33, B 31
DTO 183 ♩, 29 T

19. **Do frayg amors**
A 31, B 30
DTO 144 ♪, 47 T

20. **Du armer mensch, lass dich dein sünd hie reuen ser**
A 2, B 4
DTO 144 ♪, 56 T

21. **Du ausserweltes schöns mein herz**
A 13, B 20
DTO 183 ♩, 25 T

22. **Durch abenteuer tal und perg**
A 42, B 13
DTO 145 ♪, 66 T

23. **Durch Barbarei, Arabia**
A 49, B 19
DTO 145 ♪, 64 T

– **Durch toren weis so wird ich greis**
DTO 60 T
Melody of 31-59

24. **Erwach an, schrick, vil schönes weib**
A 51, B 17
DTO 146 ♪, 18 T

25. **Es fuegt sich, da ich was von zehen jaren alt**
A 9, B 8
DTO 146 ♪, 147 ♪, 41 T

26. **Es is ein alt gesprochen rat**
A 10
DTO 147 𝄾, 39 T; Forkel, *Geschichte der Musik*

– **Es komen neue mär greant**
DTO 73 T
Melody of 31-85

– **Es leucht durch graw die vein lasur**
DTO 34 T
Melody of 31-11

27. **Es nahent gen der vasennacht**
A 23, B 27
DTO 148 𝄾, 52 T

28. **Es seust dort her von orient**
A 11, B 10
DTO 148 𝄾, 149 𝄾, 15 T

– **Freu dich, durchleuchtig junkfrau**
A 56
DTO 83 T
Melody of 31-24

29. **Freu dich, du weltlich creatur**
A 26
DTO 185 ♩, 15 T
Wehrli 400

30. **Freuntlicher plick**
A 53, B 38
DTO 187 ♩, 19 T

31. **Fröleichen so well wir**
A 17, B 21
DTO 150 𝄾, 20 T

32. **Fröleich geschrai so well wir machen, eachen**
A 22, B 24
DTO 187 ♩, 32 T

*33. **Fröleich so will ich aber singen**
A 39, B 33
DTO 207 ♩, 231 ♪, 49 T, facsimile, frontispiece

34. **Frölich, zärtlich, lieplich und klälich, lustlich**
A 32, B 24
DTO 189 ♩, 18 T

36. **Für allen schimpf, des ich vil sich**
A 51, B 41
DTO 151 ♪, 38 T

36. **Gar wunnikleich hat si mein herz besessen**
A 25, B 28
DTO 190 ♩, 225 ♪, 25 T

37. **Gelück und hail ain michel schar**
A 23, B 27
DTO 151 ♪, 14 T

38. **Gesegent sei di frucht** (*Benedicite*)
A 5, B 7
DTO 152 ♪, 33 T

39. **Got gäb euch ainen gueten morgen**
A 41, B 34
DTO 153 ♪, 49 T

40. **Grasselick lif, war hef ick dick verloren**
B 40
DTO 191 ♩, 23 T

41. **Her wirt, uns dürstet also sere**
A 32, B 30; München Cgm 715 (*fragment*)
DTO 191 ♩, 30 T

42. **Herz, muet, leib sel und was ich han**
A 54, B 38
DTO 154 ♪, 26 T

43. **Herz, prich! rich! mich**
A 21, B 39
DTO 207 ♩, 22 T

– **Hör cristenhait**
DTO 54 T
Melody of 31-3

44. **Hört zue was ellentleicher mär**
(*Compassio Beatae Virginis Mariae*)
B 47
DTO 154 𝄾, 79 T

45. **Ich hab gehört durch mangen grans**
A 44, B 13
DTO 154 𝄾, 155 𝄾, 67 T

46. **Ich hör sich manger freuen lat**
A 38
DTO 206 𝄾, 43 T

47. **Ich klag ain engel wunneklich, innerlich**
B 44
DTO 192 ♩, 82 T (*incomplete, two lines only*)

– **Ich sich und hör**
A 3, B 12
DTO 56 T
Melody of 31-3

48. **Ich spür ain luft aus küelem tuft**
A 6, B 7
DTO 155 𝄾, 156 𝄾, 16 T
Wehrli 402

– **Ich spür ain tier**
DTO 55 T
Melody of 31-3

49. **In Frankreich**
A 7, B 6
DTO 157 𝄾, 42 T
See 31-67

50. **In Oberland**
A 57, B 45
DTO 157 𝄾, 73 T

– **In Suria ain praiten hal**
DTO 35 T
Melody of 31-11

51. **Ir alten weib, ni freut euch mit den jungen**
A 12, B 10
DTO 158 𝄾, 159 𝄾, 26 T

52. **Ir päbst, ir kaiser, du pauman**
B 47
DTO 159 𝄾, 79 T

– **Jenner besnaid Christ wirdikleich**
DTO 35 T
No melody

– **Kain ellend tet mir nie so and**
DTO 62 T
Melody of 31-59

– **Kain freud mit klarem herzen**
DTO 55 T
Melody of 31-16

– **Keuschlich geporen**
DTO 33 T
Melody of 31-17

53. **Kum liebster man!**
B 44
DTO 193 ♩, 45 T

*54. **Lieb, dein verlangen**
A 18, B 39
DTO 208 ♩, 22 T

– **Löbleicher got, gewaltikleicher**
DTO 65 T
Melody of 31-3

55. **Mein herz das ist versert**
A 30, B 28
DTO 193 ♩, 25 T

56. **Mein herz jungt sich in hoher gail**
A 30, B 29
DTO 194 ♩, 195 𝄾, 44 T

57. **Mein puel laist mir gesellschaft zwar**
A 8, B 26
DTO 160 𝄾, 14 T

58. **Mein sünd und schuld euch priester klag**
A 48, B 17
DTO 160 𝄾, 64 T

59. **Menschleichen Got, besniten schon**
A 25, B 14
DTO 160 𝄾, 36 T

– **Mich fragt ain ritter angevar**
D 85-89
DTO 75 T
No melody

60. **Mich tröst ain adeleiche maid**
A 30, B 33
DTO 195 ♩, 226 𝄾, 44 T

61. **Mir dringt czwinget**
München, Cgm 4871, p. 135
DTO 84 T
Rejected, DTO 12

62. **Mit günstlichem herzen wünsch ich dir**
A 32, B 31
DTO 196 ♩, 46 T

63. **Nempt was der schönen plüede früede**
B 43
DTO 161 𝄾, 24 T

64. **„Nu huss!" sprach der Michel von Wolkenstein**
B 36
DTO 161 ♪, 47 T
Wehrli 416

65. **Nu rue mit sorgen mein verporgenlicher schatz!**
A 19
DTO 161 ♪, 17 T

– **O herzenlieber Nickel mein**
DTO 28 T
Melody of 31-78

66. **O Pfalzgraf Ludeweig**
A 47, B 37
DTO 163 ♪, 60 T

– **O rainer got**
DTO 62 T
Melody of 31-67

67. **O snöde welt**
A 3, B 5
DTO 162 ♪, 58 T
See 31-49

68. **O welt, o welt, ain freud der kranken mauer**
A 3, B 3
DTO 163 ♪, 57 T

69. **O wunniklicher wolgezierter mai**
A 52, B 41
DTO 164 ♪, 25 T
GTM III, 17 ♩

70. **O wunnikliches paradis**
A 51, B 40
DTO 164 ♪, 38 T

– **Rot weiss, ain frölich angesicht**
B 37
DTO 44 T
Melody of 31-8

71. **Sag an, herzlieb, nu was bedeutet uns so gar**
A 17, B 22
DTO 196 ♩, 17 T

72. **Senlich we mit langer zeit und weil vertreib**
A 54, B 40
DTO 165 ♪, 45 T

73. **Sich manger freut das lange jar**
B 41
DTO 165 ♪, 71 T

74. **Sim, Gredli, Gret, traut Gredelein**
A 36, B 32
DTO 208 ♩, 232 ♪, 46 T
Wehrli 410

75. **Solt ich von sorgen werden greis**
A 22, B 26
DTO 166 ♪, 53 T

76. **Stand auff Maredel! Liebes Credel, zeuch**
A 14, B 21
Copies in Wien, Cod. 19330 *and* 19224
DTO 197 ♩, 31 T

77. **Sweig, guet gesell, schimpflichen lach**
A 40, B 34
DTO 166 ♪, 50 T

78. **Sweig still, gesell, dem ding ist recht**
A 54
DTO 167 ♪, 28 T

79. **Treib her, treib überher**
A 55, B 39
DTO 167 ♪, 29 T

80. **Tröstlicher hort, wer tröstet mich**
A 18, B 25
DTO 198 ♩, 19 T

– **Und swig ich nu die lenge zwar**
DTO 81 T
Melody of 31-59

81. **Var, heng und lass, halt in der mass**
A 7, B 8
DTO 167 ⌉, 168 ⌉, 21 T

82. **Vier hundert jar auff erd die gelten ainen tag**
A 55, B 37
DTO 199 ♩, 21 T

83. **Vil lieber grüesse süesse**
A 44, B 19
DTO 169 ⌉, 27 T, facsimile, frontispiece
See 60-3

84. **Von rechter lieb kraft**
A 23, B 27
DTO 200 ♩, 19 T; J. Wolf, *Geschichte der Mensuralnotation*, II, 139 ⌉, III, 184 ♩

85. **Von trauren möcht ich werden taub**
B 42
DTO 170 ⌉, 70 T

86. **Von Wolkenstain wolt ich zu Cölen gueter laun**
A 46, B 18
DTO 171 ⌉, 61 T

87. **Wach auff, mein hort! es leucht dort her**
A 56, B 41; Berlin 40,613, ff. 2, 71; Rostock, Univ. Bibl., ms. phil. 100/2, f. 19r
DTO 200 ♩, 17 T; SGMB 41 ♩
Lang-Salmen 70 ♩ : „Umbildung"; Müller-Blattau, in *Studien zur Musikgeschichte. Festschrift für Guido Adler* (Wien, 1930), pp. 92-99 ♩ ; Gennrich, *Melodien altd. Lieder* 14 ⌉, 20 ⌉, 21 ⌉, 24 ⌉

– **Wach, menschlich tier**
DTO 52 T
Melody of 31-3

– **Weiss, rot mit praun verleucht**
DTO 25 T
Melody of 31-55

– **Wenn ich betracht**
DTO 53 T
Melody of 31-3

88. **Wenn ich mein krank vernunft närlicher sunder**
A 5
DTO 171 𝄾, 59 T

89. **Wer die augen wil verschüren mit den prenden**
B 42
DTO 201 ♩, 72 T

90. **Wer hie umb dieser welte lust**
B 48
DTO 172 𝄾, 80 T

91. **Wer ist die da durchleuchtet**
A 4, B 6
DTO 172 𝄾, 173 𝄾, 33 T, facsimile, frontispiece

– **Wer machen well den peutel ring**
DTO 37 T
Melody of 31-23

92. **Wes mich mein puel ie hat erfreut**
A 22, B 25
DTO 173 𝄾, 61 T

– **Wie vil ich sing und tichte**
DTO 68 T
Melody of 31-16

93. **Wolauff als das zu himel sei** (*Gratias*)
A 3, B 7
DTO 152 𝄾, 33 T

94. **Wolauff, gesellen, an die vart**
A 33
DTO 174 𝄾, 36 T

95. **Wolauff gesell! wer jagen well**
A 24, B 23
DTO 202 ♩, 30 T; J. Wolf, *Geschichte der Mensuralnotation* II, 142 𝄾, III, 189 ♩

96. **Wolauff und wacht**
B 49
DTO 174 𝄾, 82 T

97. **Wolauff, wir wellen slaffen**
A 45, B 35
DTO 203 ♩, 30 T

98. **Wol auff, wolan! kind, weib und man**
A 35, B 32
DTO 204 ♩, 230 𝄾, 46 T

99. **Wol mich an we der lieben stund**
A 24, B 28
DTO 175 𝄾, 15 T

100. **Zergangen ist meins herzen we**
A 48, B 48
DTO 175 𝄾, 176 𝄾, 50 T
Wehrli 412

– **Zwar alte sünd pringt neues laid**
DTO 63 T
Melody of 31-11

101. . . . .
A 18 (no words)
DTO 209 ♩, *triplum*

102. . . . .
A 18 (no words)
DTO 209 ♩, *tenor*

32. GRAF PETER VON ARBERG

XIV C

TEBM 70; BMKH 179

1. **Ich wachter, ich solt wecken**
   „Ein ander tagwyss Graf Peters von Arberg"
   Colmar 826; Wien 2856, f. 214; Wien suppl. 3344, f. 103
   Runge, Colmar, 173 ♪
   BMKH 578

2. **Nu sterk uns Got in unser noit**
   O starcker Got, al unser not (var.)
   „*De passione Domini*"
   „Graff Peters grosse tagwyse"
   Trier, Stadtbibliothek, Hs. 724 (XV C.); Wien, Cod. membr. 7970 der K.K. Fideikommiss-bibliothek, f. 65a, 74a; Strassburg Hs. f. 111r; Colmar 828
   Runge, Colmar, 173 ♪, 175 ♪, 176 ♩, 177 ♪, facsimile, 174
   E. Bohn, in Trierer *Cäcilia*, 1877, p. 83; Bäumker, *Kath. d. Kirchlied*, I, 452; K. Bartsch and F. M. Böhme, *Germania* XXV (1880), 210 ♩; MGDM I, 176 ♩; GTM III, 16 ♩; Schirmer, *W. v. d. V.* 696, facsimile
   BMKH 579; Zitzmann 176

33. PETER VON REICHENBACH

BMKH 181

1. **Ey, froner wechter, wecke!**
   „Dyss Peter von Richenbachs hort"
   Colmar 60
   Runge, Colmar, 49 ♪, XVI ♩
   BMKH 231
   Tagelied

2. **Got, vatter, son, mit geistes fure**
   Colmar 62
   Runge, Colmar, 53 ♪
   BMKH 234
   Leich

See also 8-27

34. PETER VON SACHSEN

BMKH 184

1. **Maria gnuchtig, zuchtig**
   „Dyss ist ein barant ton her
   Peter von Sassen"
   Donaueschingen 216a-217b; Colmar 38
   Runge, Colmar, 22 ♪

– POPPE: *see* BOPPE –

35. BARTHEL REGENBOGEN

Fl. 1300

BMKH 175; TEBM 42
Hermann Kaben, *Studien zu dem Meistersinger Barthel Regenbogen.* Diss. Greifswald, 1930

1. **Den vier elmenten gab zu sture**
   „In Regenbogen gruntwysse"
   Colmar 432; APSB 48 ♩
   Runge, Colmar, 117 ♪

2. **Die erste Epistel**
   „Dunner weise"
   APSB 41 ♩

3. **Du Got der herr**
   „In dem graen don Regenbogen"
   Colmar 308; APSB 40, „Graben ton"
   Runge, Colmar, 115 ♪

4. **Du wunnenberndes süss urspring**
   „Diss ist Regenbogen geticht
   des heiligen cruczes Leich ie zwey
   lieder in einem tone sint XXII töne"
   Colmar 291; Wien 2701, f. 22b-33b
   Runge, Colmar, 106-13 ♪ ; DTO XLI, 71-77
   HM III, 389-92
   Leich
   Regenbogen *or* Frauenlob?
   See 8-55

5. **Ein edel furste botten santte**
   „Regenbogen tagewyse"
   Colmar 300; APSB 42
   Runge, Colmar, 114 ♪
   BMKH 385

6. **Ewiger, starcker, hoher, almechtiger Got**
„Dyss ist die prueffwyse die ist Frauwenlobs und Regenbogen gemein daz iglich daryn tichtet"
Colmar 244; APSB 43, „Briefe Weise"
Runge, Colmar, 105 ♪

7. **Got vatter sprach zu Abraham**
„Im Regenbogen guldin ton"
Colmar 438; APSB 47
Runge, Colmar, 118 ♪

8. **Ich singen ewig summersang**
„Hie fahent an die dryzehen reyen in der torenwise"
Colmar 283, 297
Runge, Colmar, 114 ♪
BMKH 31-32

9. **Maria, muter, reyne meyt, ein edel Gottes amme**
„In Regenbogen leyt don oder bluwend wyss"
Colmar 442; APSB 39 ♩
Runge, Colmar 118 ♪

10. **Nun will ich dir sieben jahr dienen**
„Der meisterlich Hort, in vier gekroenten Toenen... Das vierte Gesetz, im langen Ton Regenbogens"
(*Other* 3: 8-41, 9-2, 25-9
HM IV, 935 ♪; Wagenseil 554 ♪

11. **Solt ich mit hohen fuersten geuden**
„In Regenbogen langen don"
Colmar 333; APSB 38, „Der lange ton Regenbogen. Der 4 gekroenten ton einer"
Runge, Colmar 115 ♪, 116 ♪, facsimile
See 35-10
Schirmer, *W.v.d.V.* 195

See 20-6

Additional Tonen:

Braune ton, APSB 44
Süsse ton, APSB 46
Überlange ton, APSB 37

36. REINMAR VON BRENNENBERG

XIII C

BMKH 163

1. **In dyser zyt mir grossen elend ist gegeben**
   „In dem Brannenberger"
   Colmar 672
   Runge, Colmar 158 ♪

2. **Wol mich des tages dô mir alrêrst ist worden kunt**
   Kuhn-Reichert 159 ♩

37. REINMAR VON ZWETER

1200?-1260

TEBM 32, 43, 69; BMKH 159-60
G. Roethe, *Die Gedichte Reinmars von Zweter. Mit einer Notenbeilage.* Leipzig, 1887
DTO XLI

1. **Almechtig schopfer aller creature**
   „In Erenbotten spiegelwyse"
   Colmar 721; Berlin 25, p. 25; APSB 70
   Runge, Colmar 161 ♪
   BMKH 524

2. **Der Prophet Malachias spricht**
   „Erentpoden, Fürsten ton"
   APSB 68 ♩

– **Dy mynne ist gut**
  9th section of 37-4

3. **Es wont ein magt uff erden hie**
   „Her Reymar von Zwetel fraw ern don"
   Colmar 663; APSB 69 ♩,
   „Erentpoden"; Donaueschingen 233
   Runge, Colmar 155 ♪

4. **God und dyn ewen ewykit**
„Leich Reinmars von Zweter"
Wien 2701, f. 11
DTO XLI, 62 ♩
9th section:
Dy minne ist gut
Wien 2701, f. 12
DTO XLI, 63 ♩ ; NOHM II, 257 ♩

5. **Lucas im dritten der geschicht**
„Im Frauen Ehren Ton des Erenboten"
Berlin 25, p. 27
HM IV, 922 ♪

6. **Maria blüend rute**
„In Ernbotten schallwyse oder langer don"
Colmar 727
Runge, Colmar, 161 ♪

7. **„Salve regina, mater misercordie!"**
„In Rëmers sangwis von Zwetel"
Donaueschingen 227
Runge, Colmar, 184 ♪, facsimile;
Riemann 262 ♪

38. REINOLT VON DER LIPPE

1. **Min menschcit leider ist so krank**
Jena 45b
HM IV, 798 ♪ ; JHSB I, 79 ♪, II, 29 ♩
HM III, 50

38a. MEISTER REYMAR

1. **Daz eyme wol getzogenen man**
Münster fragment
SIMG XII (1910-11), 500 ♩

39. RÖMER VON ZWICKAU, MARTIN
-5 April 1483

1. **Wem ein dugentsam weib bescheret ist auff erd**
„In der gesang weiss Romers"
Berlin 25, p. 16; APSB 61
HM IV, 925 ♪
Verfasser Lexikon questions ascription

40. RUBIN
(Robyn)
XIII C

1. **Nie man ze vruo sol prisen**
   Jena 28b
   HM IV, 790 ♪ ; JHSB I, 52 ♪, II, 19 ♩
   HM III, 31

41. MEISTER RUMSLAND VON SACHSEN
2/2 XIII C

BMKH 167

1. **Aller güete voller vlüete vlôz in gnâden strâmen**
   Jena 56c
   HM IV, 803 ♪ ; JHSB I, 97 ♪, II, 34 ♩
   HM III, 61; Wehrli 448

2. **Das Gedeones wollen vlius intouwe**
   Jena 51b
   JHSB I, 89 ♪, II, 32 ♩ ; RMMA 235 ♩

3. **Der künik Nabuchodonosor sach in eime troume**
   Jena 51d
   HM IV, 801 ♪ ; JHSB I, 90 ♪, II, 33 ♩

4. **Der wise heiden Cato, der nie touf gewan**
   Jena 49b
   HM IV, 800 ♪ ; JHSB I, 85 ♪, II, 31 ♩
   HM III, 53

5. **Got herre almechtich**
   Jena 58c-59a
   HM IV, 803 ♪ ; JHSB I, 101 ♪, II, 36 ♩
   HM III, 63

6. **Got in vier elementen sich erscheint**
   Jena 47c
   HM IV, 799 ♪ ; JHSB I, 82 ♪, II, 30 ♩

7. **Herre und meister, schepfer min**
Jena 59d
HM IV, 804 ♪ ; JHSB I, 102 ♪, II, 37 ♩
HM III, 65

8. **Man fraget hoch, wo Got behuset were**
„Im geswinden ton meinster Rumsland Etlich sprechen Wolframs." *A later hand has added*: „hort dem Frawenlob zu ist sin thon"
Colmar 776
Runge, Colmar, 166 ♪
BMKH 547

9. **Ob aller minne minnen kraft**
Jena 55b
HM IV, 802 ♪ ; JHSB I, 95 ♪, II, 33 ♩
Wehrli 447
Record: Anthologie Sonore, 18

10. **Untriuwe slichet, also ein mus**
Jena 62b
HM IV, 805 ♪ ; JHSB I, 106 ♪, II, 38 ♩ ;
GTM III, 12 ♩
HM III, 67

42. RUMSLAND VON SCHWABEN

1. **Ich han nach wane dikkegelobet**
Jena 62d-63a
HM IV, 806 ♪ ; JHSB I, 107 ♪, II, 38 ♩
HM III, 68

43. DER TUGENDHAFTE SCHREIBER
XIII C

BMKH 158

1. **Ein wyser man het einen son**
„In der grüsswyse dez tugenthafften Schrybers"
Colmar 742
Runge, Colmar, 164 ♪
HM I, 364, *under* Winsbeke

44. MEISTER SINGAUF

2/2 XIII C

1. **Swer ritters namen welle enpfan**
   Jena 43d
   HM IV, 798 𝄾 ; JHSB I, 76 𝄾 , II, 28 ♩ ,
   115 ♩
   HM III, 49

45. SPERVOGEL

XII C

1. **Swâ ein vriunt dem andern vriunde bî gestat**
   Jena 29a
   HM IV, 790 𝄾 ; JHSB I, 54 𝄾 , II, 20 ♩ ;
   DAHA I, 18 ♩ ; Riemann 260 ♩
   Vogt, *Des Minnesangs Frühling*, 24

– **Swer suochet rât und volget des, der habe danc**
   Jena
   MGDM I, 156 ♩
   Vogt, *Des Minnesangs Frühling*, 20

46. DER ALTE STOLLE

TEBM 46, 71; BMKH 164
W. Seydel, *Meister Stolle nach der Jenaer Hs.* Diss. Leipzig, 1893

1. **Christus saget das himelreich**
   „In der Alment des Stollen"
   Berlin 25, p. 18
   HM IV, 921 𝄾

2. **Ich wil dich bitten, milter Got, wan du durch uns den tot**
   „In der alment des alten Stollen"
   Colmar 706; APSB 65
   Runge, Colmar, 159 𝄾 ; JHSB II, 198 ♩
   BMKH 511

3. **Lob aller engel unde lob der rechten kristenheit**
   „Meyster Stolle"
   Jena 2a
   HM IV, 775 𝄾 ; JHSB I, 2 𝄾 , II, 1 ♩
   HM III, 3

4. „Blutton", APSB 67
See 46-3

47. DER JUNGE STOLLE

TEBM 71; BMKH 168

1. **Esaias der thut beschreiben**
„Hohe ton"
APSB 66 ♩; Berlin 25, p. 21 (no words)

2. **Schaffzabel wart vor Troy herdacht**
„Dyss ist des jungen Stollen getichte"
Colmar 719
Runge, Colmar, 160 𝄾
HM II, 375; BMKH 523

48. SUCHENSINN
XIV C

TEBM 71; BMKH 181
Emil Pflug, *Suchensinn und seine Dichtungen.* Breslau, 1908.

1. **Ich kam uff einen anger wyt**
„Dyss ist in meister Suchensin tone"
Colmar 812
Runge, Colmar, 172 𝄾;
zfdA LXXX (1943-44), 97 ♩
BMKH 562

2. **Plutarchus beschreibet mit Neron**
„Im... des Suchsimsinn"
Berlin 24, f. 157r

49. TANNHÄUSER
1205?-1270

BMKH 162; TEBM 40
A. Oehlke, *Zu Tannhäusers Leben und Dichten.* Diss. Königsberg, 1890.
Johannes Siebert, *Der Dichter Tannhäuser, Leben, Gedichte, Sage.* 1934.
Margarete Lang, *Tannhäuser.* Leipzig, 1936.
Tannhäuserlied
„Welle grosse wunder schauen will," Schweizer Volkslied, HM IV, 936 ♩; Franz M. Böhme, *Altdeutsches Liederbuch.* Leipzig, Breitkopf u. Härtel, 1877, p. 86 ♩. „Wolt wir aber haben an", Böhme 82 𝄾.

1. **Ez ist hiute ein wunniklicher tak**
Jena 42d
HM IV, 797 ; JHSB I, 74 , II, 27 ;
NOHM II, 254
HM III, 48

2. **Gelückes wer mir not**
„In Tanhusers heuptton oder guldin tone"
Colmar 785; Berlin 25, p. 359
Runge, Colmar 169 ; JHSB II, 200

– **Ich lobe ein wip, diu ist noch bezzer danne guot**
German text to 49-4
HM II, 85-87

3. **Mir tet gar wol ein lieber wan**
„Des Danhusers lude leich"
Colmar 72
Runge, Colmar, 64
BMKH 245-51

4. **Syon egredere nunc de cubilibus**
München 5539, ff. 161-67
Spanke, ZfMW XIV (1931-32), 385-97 ; ZfdA LXIX (1932), 49-70; Hugo Kuhn, *Minnesangs Wende* (Tübingen, Niemeyer, 1952), 164-70, facsimile
German text: Ich lobe... *above*

5. „Hofton", APSB 97

50. ULRICH VON WINTERSTETTEN

Fl. 1240-1280

J. Minor, *Die Leiche und Lieder des Schenken Ulrich von Winterstetten.* 1882
A. Selge, *Studien über Ulrich von Winterstetten* (German Studien LXXI, 1929)

1. **Diu minne stoeret unde toeret mich ân allen wân**
Schreibers fragment (lost)
Facsimile in Kuhn, *Minnesangs Wende* (*see* 49-4), 164; Schreiber, *Taschenbuch für Geschichte und Altertum in Süddeutschland.*
KLD 503-508, Leich IV, „Swer die wunne, *of which* Diu minne... *is line* 53 (p. 505)

– **Ich möhte ersterben sol min werben niht erschiezen mir**
Line 51 of Leich IV
Kuhn-Reichert 160 ♩

51. DER UNGELEHRTE

Fl. 1300?

TEBM 46, 71; BMKH 166

1. **Sang ist ein wyse meinsterschaft**
„In dem Ungelarten"
Colmar 750
Runge, Colmar, 164 𝄾

52. DER UNVERZAGTE

2/2 XIII C

1. **Der künik Ruodolf minnet Got und ist an triuwen staete**
Jena 40d
HM IV, 795 𝄾, 860f ♩; MGDM I, 168 ♩; RMMA 234 ♩; GTM III, 11 ♩; JHSB I, 70 𝄾, II, 26 𝄾; GMMA 222 ♩; HGEM 21 ♩; Moser, *Minnesang und Volkslied* (Leipzig, 1929), 17
HM III, 45
Record: Decca 20158

2. **Ez ist ein lobeliche kunst**
Jena 40a
HM IV, 795 𝄾; JHSB I, 69 𝄾, II, 25 ♩; GMMA 222 ♩
HM III, 44

3. **Junger man von zweinzik jaren**
Jena 39b
HM IV, 794 𝄾; JHSB I, 68 𝄾, II, 24 ♩; GFML 192 ♩
HM III, 43

53. VEGEVIUR

Verfasser Lexikon IV, 682

1. **Maria, muoter unde maghet**
   Basel N.J. 3, nr. 145
   Spruchstrophe

54. WALTHER VON DER VOGELWEIDE

1170?-1230?

BMKH 156

Die Gedichte Walthers von der Vogelweide, zwölfte Ausgabe, (Karl Lachmann) ed. Carl v. Kraus. Berlin, De Gruyter, 1959.
Walther von der Vogelweide, *Sprüche, Lieder, der Leich*. Berlin, Tempel, 1955.
Walther von der Vogelweide, *Die Gedichte*. Berlin, De Gruyter, 1955.
Friedrich Maurer, *Die Lieder Walthers von der Vogelweide*. I, *Die religiösen und die politischen Lieder*, 1955. II. *Die Liebeslieder*. Tübingen, Niemeyer, 1955-56.
Karl-Heinz Schirmer, *Die Strophik Walthers von der Vogelweide*. Halle, Niemeyer, 1956.
Kienast, „Walthers ältester Spruch im Reichston," *Gymnasium* LVII, 201 ff.
R. Wustmann, „Die Hofweise Walthers von der Vogelweide," *Liliencron Festschrift*, pp. 440-63. Leipzig, 1910.
Friedrich Pfaff, *Der Minnesang des 12. bis 14. Jahrhunderts*. Abteilung 2.
Friedrich Gennrich, „Zur Liedkunst Walthers von der Vogelweide," zfdA LXXXV (1954-55), 203-09.
Fr. Pfeiffer, „Zwei Lieder Walthers von der Vogelweide," *Germania* II (1857), 470 ff.
K. Plenio, „Die Überlieferung Waltherscher Melodien," *PB Beitr.* XLII, 479-90.
Carl von Kraus, *Walther von der Vogelweide, Untersuchungen*. Berlin, De Gruyter, 1935.
Rudolph Wustmann, „Walthers Palaestinalied," SIMG XIII (1911-12), 247-50.
C. Bützler, *Untersuchungen zu den Melodien Walthers von der Vogelweide* (Deutsche Arbeiten der Universität Köln, Nr. 12). Jena, 1940, Pp. 112.
Friedrich Gennrich, „Melodien Walthers von der Vogelweide," zfdA LXXXI (1942), 24-28.
J. A. Huisman, *Neue Wege zur dichterischen und musikalischen Technik Walther von der Vogelweide* (Studia Litteraria Rheno-Traiectina, I). Utrecht, 1950.
Wolfgang Mohr, „Zu Walthers 'Hofweise' und 'Feinem Ton'", zfdA LXXXV (1954-55), 38-43.

1. **Am dreizehenden sein Mathei sagt Christus**
„In Creuz Ton Walter von der Vogelweid"
Berlin 25, p. 12

2. **Das ein und sechzigste Caputt Esaie**
„Feine ton"
APSB 58
Wustmann, *op. cit.*; Bützler 66 ♪
Ascription: *see* 54-11

– **Allerest leb' ich...**: *see* *21, *below*

3. **Die trinitat gedryet**
„In her Walthers guldin wyse"
Colmar 736
Runge, Colmar, 163 ♪; Bützler 50 ♪, facsimile

4. **Diu menscheit muoz verderben**
See 54-12, 26

5. **Diu welt was gelf, rot unde blâu**
Melody of Gautier d'Espinal, Amours et bone volentés
zfdA LXXIX, 46 ♩

*6. **Friuntlichen lac ein ritter vil gemeit**
„Walthers Tagelied"
Maurer II, 135 ♩; zfdA LXXIX, 38 ♩; Gennrich, *Mhd. Liedkunst* 12 ♪
Schirmer 200

7. **Frô Welt, ir sult dem wirte sagen**
Melody of Blondel de Nesle, Onques nus hom ne chanta
zfdA LXXIX, 47 ♩; Gennrich, *Mhd. Liedkunst* 17 ♪

8. **Got gît ze künege swener wil**
Bützler 68 ♪
See 54-2

*9. **Her babest, ich mac wol genessen**
„Der Ottenton"
Aarburg, *op. cit.*; APSB 58 (p. 175a)
GTM III, 6a ♩ ; Bützler 73 ⌉ ; Gennrich, *Mhd. Liedkunst* 13 ⌉ ; contrafactum: APSB 58 (p. 175a)
Wustmann 444; Maurer I, 50 ♩
See 54-10

*10. **Her keiser, sit ir willekomen**
(March, 1212)
„Der Ottenton"
Maurer I, 49 ♩ ; zfdA LXXIX, 39 ♩
Wehrli 218
See 54-9

11. **Hie hört wie in der Apostel Geschicht**
„In des H: Johannis Walters tön 3. Ein Landherr"
„Lange ton"
APSB 56 ♩ (p. 172b); Bützler 64, facsimile, 95 ⌉, *under* „unechte Melodien"

12. **Ich freu mich des das mir**
Ascription: *see* 54-11
„Creuzton"
APSB 57 ♩ (p. 174a); Bützler 75 ⌉
See 54-4

*13. **Ich horte ein wazzer diezen**
„Der Reichston"
Maurer I, 28; zfdA LXXIX, 43 ♩
Kraus 10

*14. **Ich saz uf eime steine** (*ca.* 1198-1201)
„Der Reichston"
Maurer I, 27 ♩
Wehrli 208

15. **Maneger klaget die schoenen zît**
Bützler 62 ♩
See 54-3

16. **Mary, du bist daz bernde ryss**
„Her Walthers von der Vogelweyde hoffwyse oder wendelwys"
Colmar 734
Runge, Colmar, 162 𝄾 ; ZfdA LXXIX, 34 ♩ ; Bützler 40 𝄾 , facsimile, 46-47 𝄾
HM I, 257-60
See 54-24, 28

*17. **Mir hat ein lieht von Franken**
(*ca.* 1207-08)
Münster fragment
SIMG XII (1910-11), 500 ♩ ;
MGDM I, 161 ♩ Bützler 8 𝄾, 14-15 ♩ ;
ZfdA LXXIX, 29 ♩ ; Maurer, I, 43 ♩
Tempel edn., 17; DeGruyter, 145
Maurer: „Der zweite Philippston"

*18. **Mir hat her Gerhart Atze ein pfert erschozzen z Isenache**
(before 1207)
„Der erste Atzeton"
Maurer, I, 41 ♩ ; ZfdA LXXIX, 42 ♩

*19. **Mit saelden müeze ich hiute ufsten**
(*ca.* 1206)
„Der Wiener hofton"
Maurer, I, 33 ♩
See 54-28

*20. **Muget ir schouwen waz dem meien**
Melody of Gautier d'Espinal, Quant je voi l'erbe menue; Carmina Burana, nr. 151, 169 (f. 61r): *see* Bützler 105
Maurer II, 57 ♩ ; ZfdA LXXIX, 47 ♩

*21. **Nu alerst leb' ich mir werde**
„Palestina Lied" (1228)
Münster fragment
SIMG XII (1910-11), 499 ♩ ; MGDM I, 162 ♩ ; SGMB 6 ♩ ; RMMA 234 ♩ ;
NOHM II, 253 ♩ ; DTO XLI, 87 ♩ ; Adler,

Handbuch der Musikgeschichte I, 2, 204 ♩; GFML 247 ♩ ; GTM III, 6b ♩ ; GMMA 219 ♩ ;DAHA I, 18 ♩ ; SIMG XIII (1911-12), 247-50; HGEM 20 ♩ ; *Z.f.d. Bildung* II (1926), 630; Huisman 147; Maurer I, 15 ♩ ; H. Husmann, *Die Musikforschung* VI (1953), 17 ♩ ; ZfMW VII, 98 ♩ ; ZfdA LXXIX, 32 ♩; A. A. Abert, *Musikforschung* I (1948), 103ff.; Gennrich, *Mhd. Liedkunst* 16 ⌉ ; Bützler 26 ⌉, 28 ♩, 29 ♩, 34 ♩ ; *Melody of* Jaufré Rudel, Lanquan li jorn son long en mai: *see* GTM 51
Tempel 78; De Gruyter 271
Records:Decca 20158; Anthologie Sonore 18

*22. **Philippe, künic here**
„Der zweite Philippston"
GTM III, 6c ♩ ; *Z. f. d. Bildung* II (1926), 631; Maurer I, 44 ♩ ; Gennrich, *Mhd. Liedkunst* 14 ⌉
Studi Medievali XVII (1951), 71-85
See 54-17

*23. **Sie wunderwol gemachet wip**
Kremsmünster, Stiftsbibliothek, Ms. 127, VII, 18, f. 130r
Maurer II, 96 ♩

24. **Swer houbet sünde unt schande**
ZfdA LXXIX, 36 ♩ ; Bützler 47 ⌉
See 54-16

25. **Uns hât der winter geschât über al**
Melody of Moniot de Paris,
Quant voi ces prés florir et verdoier
ZfdA LXXIX, 46 ♩

26. **Vil süeze waere minne**
„Walters Kreuzlied"
Bützler 79 ♩
See 54-4, 54-12

*27. **Vil wol gelobter Got, wie selten ich dich prîse!** (1212-13)
„Die könig Friedrichston"
Münster fragment
Maurer I, 54 ♩; SIMG XII (1910-11), 499 ♩; MGDM I, 161 ♩; SGMB 7 ♩; Bützler 16 ⌉, 23 ♩
BMKH 536
Line 8: Wie solte ich den geminnen

*28. **Waz wunders in der werlte vert**
„Der Wiener Hofton"
GTM III, 6d ♩; Bützler 40 ⌉, 49 ♩; Mantuani, *Geschichte der Musik in Wien* I, 299; Gennrich, *Mhd. Liedkunst* 11 ⌉
Maurer I, 35
See 54-16, 24

– **Wie solte ich den geminnen**: 54-27

*29. **Wol mich der stunde, daz ich sie erkunde**
Melody of Bernart de Ventadorn, Can vei la flor, l'erba e la folha
Maurer II, 89 ♩; ZfdA LXXIX, 45 ♩; Gennrich, *Mhd. Liedkunst* 16 ⌉; Moser, ZfMW XVI (1934), 150f; ZfMW LXXXVII, 43.

See also 60-2

– DER WARTBURG KRIEG –

See 10-1, 18-1, 57 I
and *Verfasser Lexikon* IV, 843-64; HM II, 1-19, III, 170-82

55. BRUDER WERNER

XIII C

A. Schönbach, *Die Sprüche Bruder Werner* (Sitzungsberichte der Akademie der Wissenschaft zu Wien, Phil.-his. Klasse, 1904, nr. 7; 1905, nr. 6)

1. **Ich buwe ein hus, da inne wil gesinde wesen**
Jena 14d
HM IV, 778 ⌉; JHSB I, 27 ⌉, II, 6 ♩
HM III, 19

2. **Ich weiz der herren manigen ob ich het ir eines guot**
Jena 12c
JHSB I, 23 𝄾, II, 4 ♩; HM IV, 777

3. **Nu merket, wa ein blinder get**
Jena 14a
HM IV, 778 𝄾; JHSB I, 26 𝄾, II, 5. ♩

4. **Nu schouwet an den sumer guot**
Jena 9b
HM IV, 776 𝄾; JHSB I, 17 𝄾, II, 3 ♩, 117 ♩

5. **Swer sich mit vremden liuten wil**
Jena 15d
HM IV, 779 𝄾; JHSB I, 29 𝄾, II, 7 ♩

6. **Wir lan die pfaffen sin vertan**
Jena 7d
HM IV, 775 𝄾; JHSB I, 12 𝄾, II, 2 ♩
HM III, 11

56. WIZLAV (III, FÜRST) VON RÜGEN
1265?-1325

Ludwig Ettmüller, *Wizlavs Sprüche und Lieder* (Bibl. der d. nat. Literatur XXXIII), 1852.
E. Gülzow, *Des Fürsten Wizlaw von Rügen Minnelieder und Sprüche*, 1922.
A. Dölling, *Die Lieder Wizlaws* III *von Rügen, klanglich und musikalisch untersucht*. Diss. Leipzig, 1926.
Friedrich Gennrich, „Zu den Melodien Wizlavs von Rügen," ZfdA LXXX (1943-44), 86-102.
R. J. Taylor, „A Song by Prince Wizlav of Rügen," *Modern Language Review* XLVI (1951), 31-37.

1. **Der herbest kumt uns riche genuoch**
Jena 80d
HM IV, 817 𝄾; JHSB I, 135 𝄾, II, 52 ♩
HM III, 85; PMDL I, 249

2. **Der Ungelarte heft gemaket**
Jena 75c
HM IV, 811 𝄾; JHSB I, 127 𝄾, II, 45 ♩;
Lang-Salmen 64 ♩
HM III, 81

3. **Der walt unde anger lit gebreit**
   Jena 79a
   HM IV, 815 ♪ ; JHSB I, 132 ♪ , II, 50 ♩ ;
   MGDM I, 171 ♩ ; Riemann 268 ♩
   HM III, 84

4. **Diu erde ist entslozzen**
   Jena 77d
   HM IV, 813 ♪ ; JHSB I, 130 ♪ , II, 48 ♩ ;
   Riemann 268 ♩
   HM III, 82

5. **Diu vogelin**
   Jena 79d
   HM IV, 816 ♪ ; JHSB I, 134 ♪ , II, 51 ♩ ;
   GFML 207 ♩
   HM III, 84

6. **Ich parrere dich durch mine trowe**
   Jena 75a
   HM IV, 810 ♪ , 860f ♩ ; JHSB I, 127 ♪ ,
   II, 44 ♩ ; NOHM II, 253 ♩ ; Lang-Salmen 62 ♩
   HM III, 81

7. **Ich warne dich, vil junger man gezarte**
   Jena 77a
   HM IV, 813 ♪ ; JHSB I, 129 ♪ , II, 47 ♩
   HM III, 82
   Incomplete

8. **List du in der minne dro**
   Jena 77a
   HM IV, 812 ♪ ; JHSB I, 129 ♪, II, 47 ♩ ;
   GTM III, 15d ♩ ; Riemann, 271 ♩ ;
   GFML 239 ♩ ; GMMA 223 ♩
   HM III, 81-82

9. **Löuvere risen von den bômen hin to dal**
   Jena 80b
   HM IV, 816 ♪, 860f ♩ ; GTM III, 15c ♩ ;
   F. Gennrich, „Liedkontrafactur
   in mhd. und ahd. Zeit," ZfdA
   LXXXII (1948), 134 ♩ ;
   Riemann, 269 ♩ ; JHSB I, 134 ♪ , II, 51
   HM III, 85

10. **Manik schimpfet uf sin eigen zil**
Jena 76c
HM IV, 812 ♪ ; JHSB I, 128 ♪, II, 46 ♩ ;
Lang-Salmen 66 ♩
HM III, 81

11. **Meije schoene, kum jo zuo**
Jena 78d
HM IV, 815 ♪ ; JHSB I, 132 ♪, II, 49 ♩
HM III, 83 ; PMDL I, 248

12. **Menschen kind, denket dar an**
Jena 73a
HM IV, 809 ♪ ; JHSB I, 124 ♪, II, 42 ♩
HM III, 78

13. **Nach der senenden klage muoz ich singhen**
Jena 76b
HM IV, 811 ♪ ; ZfdA LXXX, 87 ♩ ; 94 ♩
GTM III, 15a ♩ ; JHSB I, 128 ♪, II, 46 ♩ ;
Gennrich, *Mhd. Liedkunst* 21 ♪ ; MLR XLVI, 31 ♪-37 ♩
HM III, 81

14. **O we, ich han gedacht**
Jena 77c
HM IV, 813 ♪ ; JHSB I, 130 ♪, II, 47 ♩ ;
GMMA 218 ♩ ; GTM III, 15b ♩ ; MGDM I, 170 ♩ ; HGEM 20 ♩ ; Gennrich, *Mhd. Liedkunst* 21 ♪
HM III, 82
Record: Decca 20158

15. **Sage an, du boser man**
Jena 74c
HM IV, 809 ♪ ; JHSB I, 126 ♪, II, 43 ♩
HM III, 80

– **We, ich han gedacht: O we...**

16. **Wol dan, her meije, ich gibe iuch des die hulde**
Jena 79c
HM IV, 815 ♪; JHSB I, 133 ♪, II, 50 ♩
HM III, 84

17. **Wol uf, ir stolzen helde**
Jena 78a
HM IV, 814 ♪; JHSB I, 131 ♪, II, 48 ♩;
MGDM I, 169 ♩
HM III, 83; PMDL I, 246

57. WOLFRAM VON ESCHENBACH
Fl. 1200-1220

BMKH 157
Wolfram von Eschenbach, ed. Albert Leitzmann. Halle, Niemeyer, 1926.
Lieder: Heft V, 179-87.

1. **Als Christus wandeln thete**
„Wolff Rones eines Ritter"
„Kreuzton"
APSB 50 ♩

2. **Als Gott saget zu Abraham**
„Wolff Rones eines Ritter"
„Lange ton"
APSB 49 ♩; MGDM I, 316 ♩

3. **Do man dem edelen sin gezelt**
„Im swarzen don"
„Kriek von Wartberk"
Jena 127d
HM IV, 844 ♪; JHSB I, 221 ♪, II, 84 ♩
HM III, 171

4. **Hoseas der heylig Prophet**
„Wolff Rones eines Ritter"
„Flamm weise"
APSB 53 ♩

5. **Jamer ist mir entsprungen**
Wien, Titurel Hs. 40
HM IV, 774, facsimile; MGDM I, 163 ♩

6. **Jeremias weissaget**
„Wolff Rones eines Ritter"
„Vergolten ton"
APSB 54 ♩
Nuremberg 784 ♩, 792 ♩, *under*
APSB 54

7. **Matheus schreibt am achten Christus drat in ein schiff**
„In der Honn' weiss Wolframs"
Berlin 25, p.1
HM IV, 921 ♪

8. **Was sol ein keyser one recht**
„In Wolframs guldin tone von Eschelbach"
Colmar 730
Runge, Colmar 162 ♪; APSB 52
HM II, 260; BMKH 535

9. „Hohe weise"
APSB 55

10. „Kurze ton"
APSB 51

58. MEISTER ZILIES VON SAYN

1. **Ein kupfer so verguldet was, daz ez gar guldin shein**
Jena 21a
HM IV, 783 ♪; JHSB I, 39 ♪, II, 11 ♩
HM III, 25

2. **So wol dem hobe, da man triuwe an hoher wirde hat**
Jena 20c
HM IV, 782 ♪; JHSB I, 38 ♪, II, 10 ♩;
GTM III, 10 ♩
HM III, 25

59. ZWINGER

2/2 XIV C

BMKH 182

1. **Adam und Even schuld wart hart uns armen**
   „In des Zwingers rotten don, sin hort"
   Colmar 79; APSB 86
   Runge, Colmar, 66 ♪

2. „Hofton", APSB 85.

60. ANONYMOUS

1. **Ich han vor lorin den lybyster bulen myn**
   Wien 2701
   DTO XLI, 62 ♩

2. **Ich setze minen vuz (fuoz)**
   Magdeburger Archiv
   Berlin 981
   HM IV, 773, facsimile; NOHM II, 255 ♩; Wolf, *Handbuch der Notationskunde* I, 176 ♩, facsimile; Wolf, *Musikalische Schrifttafeln*, pl. 21, facsimile;
   Kuhn-Reichert 157 ♩
   KLD I, 277

3. **Man sieht lawber tawer**
   Vipiteno 35b-36a
   Zingerle, *Wien Sitzungsberichte*... LIV, 324ff; DTO XVIII, 108
   Umdichtung of Jam entrena plena: *see* 31-83

4. **...sin hanne genommen**
   Münster fragment
   SIMG XII, 498 ♩; Bützler 99-101 ♪
   „Neue Ton" *of* Walther von der Vogelweide? *See* Bützler 99-102

5. **Rôsen ûf der heide mit leide**
   Erlangen 13b
   Kuhn-Reichert 157 ♩

6. **Wat den bin ic? ein spilemen**
Karl Bartsch's XIII c. ms.
fragment (*lost?*)
Erk-Böhme, *Deutsche Liederhort*
(Leipzig, 1925), II, 189, 376:
„mit zweifelhaft übertragener
Melodie", Lang-Salmen, 123.
Lang-Salmen 72

61. MINNESINGER, TROUBADOURS, TROUVÈRES

An increasing attention to musical and literary relationships between these three has produced, among others, the groups of related poems below, together with the following bibliography:
Ursula Aarburg, *op. cit. supra*; K. Bartsch, in *Germania* I (1856), 480-82; O. Schultz-Gora, ZfdA XXI (1887), 185-89; C. von Kraus, *Untersuchungen*; F. Michel, *Heinrich von Morungen und die Troubadours* (Quellen und Forschungen XXXVIII), 1880; F. Gennrich, „Der deutsche Minnesang in seinem Verhältnis zur Troubadour- und Trouvère-Kunst", *Z.f.d. Bildung* II (1926), 536-68, 622-32; F. Gennrich, „Sieben Melodien zu mittelhochdeutschen Minneliedern," ZfMW VII (1924-25), 65-98; H. Spanke, „Romanische und mittellateinische Formen in der Metrik von Minnesangs Frühling," ZfrP XLIX (1929), 190-235; H. Spanke, *Beziehungen zwischen romanischer und mittellateinischer Lyrik* (Abhandlungen der Göttinger Ges. d. Wiss., Phil.-Hist. Klasse, 3. Folge, Nr. 18), 1936; H. J. Moser, „Zu Ventadorns Melodien," ZfMW XVI (1934), 150ff.
István Frank, *Trouvères und Minnesänger*. 2 vols., Saarbrücken, 1952, 1956. Vol. I. Recueil de Textes; II, Kritische Ausgaben der Weisen... von Wendelin Müller-Blattau.
See also 54, Walther von der Vogelweide.

ALBRECHT VON JOHANSDORF

1. **Ich vant âne huote**
Un Marquis, Dona a vos me coman
Frank I, 86-91, *no melody*

BERNGER VON HORHEIM

2. **Mir ist alle zît als ich vliegende var**
Anon., Puis ke li mal k'Amours me font sentir
Bertran de Born, Miez sirventes vueilh far dels reis amdos
Frank I, 92-97, II, 91 ♪

3. **Nu lange ich mit sange die zît hân gekündet**
Gace Brulé, Ne puis faillir a bone chançon fere
Frank I, 108-11, II, 103 ♪

4. **Wie solt ich armer der swaere getrûwen**
Conon de Bethune, Moult me semont Amors ke je m'envoise
Bertran de Born, Ai, Lemozis, francha terra cortesa
Bertran de Born, Pois als baros enoja e lur pesa
Gace Brulé, Bien ait l'amor dont l'en cuide avoir joie
Frank I, 98-107, II, 94-100 𝄾

DIETMAR VON EIST

5. **Der winter waere mir ein zît**
Heinrich von Rugge, Hân ich iht vriunt, die wünschen ir
Pseudo-Veldeke, Swenn diu zît alsô gestât
Bernart de Ventadorn, Quan vei l'alauzeta mover
GTM 45 ♩ ; Gennrich, *Mhd. Liedkunst* 6 𝄾

FRIEDRICH VON HUSEN

6. **Deich von der guoten sehiet**
Bernart de Ventadorn, Pos prejatz me, senhor
Frank I, 2-5, II, 9-10 𝄾 ; ZfMW VII, 92 ♩ ; GTM 46 ♩ ;
HGEM 20 ♩

7. **Diu süezen wort hânt mir getân**
Bernger von Horheim, Nu enbeiz ich doch des trankes nie
Chrestien de Troyes, D'Amors qui m'a tolu a moy
Gaucelm Faidit, Si tot m'a tarzat mon chan
Frank I, 22-27, II, 33-34 𝄾 ; ZfMW VII, 96 ♩ ; GTM 49 ♩

8. **Gelebt ich noch die lieben zît**
Blondel de Nesle, Se savoient mon tourment

9. **Ich denke under wîlen**
Guiot de Provins, Ma joie premeraine
Vidame de Chartres, Combien que j'ai demouré
Frank I, 16-21, II, 87 𝄾 ; GTM 47 ♩ ; Gennrich, *Mhd. Liedkunst* 10 𝄾 ;
GFML 197-98 ♩

10. **Ich lobe Got der sîner güete**
Gace Brulé, Pensis d'Amors voil retraire
Frank I, 10-15, II, 23-24 𝄾

11. **Mîn herze den gelouben hât**
Gontier de Soignies, Tant ai mon chant entrelaissié
Gontier de Soignies, Se li oisel baissent lor chans

12. **Mîn herze und mîn lîp diu wellent scheiden**
Albrecht von Johansdorf, Mich mac der tôt
Conon de Bethune, Ahi, Amors, com dure departie
Chastelain de Coucy, La douce vois du rossignol salvage
Frank I, 28-33, II, 40-46 ♪ ; ZfMW VII, 94 ♩

13. **Mir ist daz herze wunt**
Anon., Mult m'a demoré
Frank I, 6-9, II, 16-17 ♪ ; GTM 46 ♩

14. **Si waenent sich dem tôde verzîn**
Anon., El dous tens que voi venir
No melody

HARTMANN VON AUE

15. **Ich muoz von rehte den tac iemer minnen**
Gace Brulé, Ire d'amors ke en mon cuer repaire
Frank I, 126-30, II, 116 ♩, 117 ♪

HEINRICH VON MORUNGEN

16. **Lanc bin ich geweset verdâht**
(*Authorship?*)
Anon., Je ne sui pas esbahis
Frank I, 116-19, II, 109 ♪

17. **Mirst geschên als eime kindelîne**
Anon., Aissi m'ave cum a l'enfant petit
Frank I, 112-15, *no melody*

HEINRICH VON VELDEKE

18. **Als die vogele frewelîche**
Bernart de Ventadorn, Bel m'es quant eu vei la broilla
Richart de Semilli, Quant la sesons renouvele
Richart de Semilli, De chanter m'est pris courage

19. **Ich bin frô, sît uns die tage**
Pierre de Molins(?), Fine amours et bone esperance

20. **Sî is sô gût ende ouch so scône**
Gace Brulé, Pour mal temps ne por gelee
Frank I, 34-39, *no melody*

21. **Swer zer minne ist sô fruot**
Gace Brulé, Oiés pour quoi plaing et soupir

PSEUDO-REIMAR

22. **Mîn ougen wurden liebes also vol**
Gaucelm Faidit, Mon cor e mi e mas bonas chansos

RUDOLF VON FENIS

23. **Gewan ich ze Minnen ie guoten wân**
Folquet de Marselha, Sitot me soi a tart aperceubutz
Folquet de Marselha, Tant m'abellis l'amoros pessamens
Folquet de Marselha, S'al cor plagues, ben for' oimais sazos
Frank I, 46-55, II, 64 ⌉ ; ZfMW VII, 75 ♩, 77 ♩ ; GTM 48 ♩

24. **Minne gebiutet daz ich singe**
Gace Brulé, De bone amor et de loial amie
Frank I, 56-61, II, 66-71 ⌉ ; ZfMW VII, 87 ♩ ; Gennrich, *Mhd. Liedkunst* 8 ⌉

25. **Mit sange wânde ich mîne sorge krenken**
Ich hân mir selben gemachet die swaere
Friedrich von Husen, Si darf mich des zîhen niet
Hartwig von Rute, Mir tuot ein sorge wê in mînen muote
Bligger von Steinach, Er fünde guoten kouf an mînen jâren
Folquet de Marselha, En chantan m'aven a membrar
Folquet de Marselha, Ben ant mort mi e lor
Gaucelm Faidit, Pel messatgier que fai tan lonc estage
Gace Brulé, Merci, Amours, qu'iert il de mon martire
Gace Brulé, Tant m'ait meneit force de signoraige
Hugues de Bregi, Ausi con cil qui cuevre sa pesance
Anon., Je ne mi vueil de bone amour retraire
Anon., Espris d'amour et de longue atendance
Anon., Ce qu'Amours a si tres grande poissance
Frank I, 62-79, II, 72-84 ⌉ ; ZfMW VII, 89 ♩ ; GTM 45 ♩ ; Gennrich, *Mhd. Liedkunst* 7 ⌉

26. **Nun ist niht mêre mîn gedinge**
Swer sô staeten dienest kunde
Peire Vidal, Pos tornatz sui em Proensa
Frank I, 80-85, II, 87 ⌉ ; ZfMW VII, 78-79 ♩ ; GTM 49 ♩

ULRICH VON GUTENBERG

27. **Ich hôrte wol ein merlikîn singen**
Blondel de Nesle, Bien doit chanter qui fine Amors adreche
Frank I, 40-45, II, 55-58 ⌉ ; GTM 47 ♩ ; GFML 221-22 ♩

62. CARMINA BURANA

See Aarburg, *op.cit*; H. Spanke, „Der *Codex Buranus* als Liederbuch," ZfMw XIII (1931), 241 ff.; W. Lipphardt, „Unbekannte Weisen zu den Carmina Burana," AfMw XII (1955), 122 ff.; also 54, Walther von der Vogelweide.

Included in the *Carmina Burana* are the following tunes, in staffless neumes:

1. Pseudo-Dietmar, Urlop hât des sumers brehen
   CB 161-161a
2. Heinrich von Morungen, Ich bin keiner âne krône
   CB 150a (f. 61r), *incomplete*
3. Reimar, Sage, daz ich dirs iemer lône
   CB 147a (f. 60v)
4. Pseudo-Reimar, Sold ab ich mit sorgen iemer leben
   CB 166-166a
5. Pseudo-Reimar, Ze niuwen fröuden stât mîn muot
   CB 143a (f. 59r)

CHRONOLOGY

XII Century

45

XIII Century

1, 3, 4, 6, 8, 10, 14, 17, 18, 20, 25, 27, 30, 36, 37, 40, 41, 43, 44, 49, 50, 52, 53, 54, 55, 57

XIV Century

2, 7, 9, 13, 16, 19, 21, 22, 26, 28, 32, 33, 35, 48, 51, 56, 58, 59

XV Century

15, 29, 31, 39

The Four Gekrönte Töne: 8-13, 8-41, 9-2, 25-8, 25-9, 35-10, 35-11
See TEBM 60-61

The Twelve Masters:

1. Herr Walter ein Landherr, von der Fogel weid
2. Wolffgang Rohn ein Ritter
3. Conrat Marner ein Edelman
4. D: Henrich Frauenlob zu Menz } D: teologie
5. D: Henrich Mugeling }
6. M: Klingesohr
7. M: Starcke Popp
8. Bartel Regenbogen, ein Schmid
9. Der Römer war von Zwickau, ein burger
10. Der Kanzeler war ein fischer
11. Conrad von Wirzberg
12. Der allte Stoll

List from: Adam Puschmann, *Gruntlicher Bericht des deutschen Meister Gesanges*, 1584